Great Mysteries of the Bible

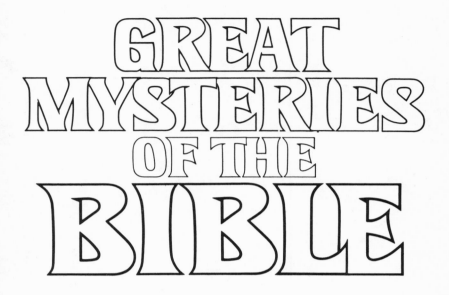

GREAT MYSTERIES OF THE BIBLE

John R. Bisagno

BROADMAN PRESS
Nashville, Tennessee

© Copyright 1981 • Broadman Press
All rights reserved.

4219-52

ISBN: 0-8054-1952-7

Dewey Decimal Classification: 252
Subject heading: SERMONS — COLLECTIONS
Library of Congress Catalog Card Number: 81-67997
Printed in the United States of America

DEDICATION

To
my beloved associate pastor
Felix Wagner
whose coshepherding of First Baptist Church
enables me to spend the time in study and prayer
to pursue the mysterious and wonderful ways
of God revealed in his glorious Word

Contents

1
The Mystery of Hidden Things

We shall, in these pages, attempt to address ourselves to a clearer understanding of God. Admittedly, there is much of God that may not be learned in this life. The result of sin is, in part, separation from a clear understanding of the perfect knowledge of God. It is, however, a shortcoming that shall be gloriously resolved at the glorification of the believer when "we shall be like him; for we shall see him as he is" (1 John 3:2). Until that time, however, it is clear that much is hidden from man.

The Scriptures speak of many great mysteries — things hard to understand, and even impossible to fully comprehend in this life. It behooves us, however, to give our best effort at arriving at all of the understanding of truth that God is willing to make available unto us.

Far from chastising God for his unwillingness to reveal all things to us now, we should, rather, rejoice in amazement that God has chosen to make any of his marvelous ways known to the sons of man. Yet our Lord not only chooses to do so but also has, through the centuries, even broadened the revelation of himself and his ways to the human race.

That we know anything of God — that he wants us to know anything of himself — is, indeed, a marvelous and wonderful mystery to comprehend. It is a glorious truth that God not only wills to reveal his ways to people but also actually takes the initiative in doing so. Yet with it all, there is much that may not be fully comprehended until we arrive at last in heaven by his grace. Nonetheless, wise believers will give themselves in the pursuit of the knowledge of all the mysteries of God — with the support of the Holy Spirit who "searcheth ... the deep things of God."

A positive mind-set is essential as we begin our journey toward a broadened understanding of the ways of God. Keep firmly in mind that God is more eager for you to know his will than you are to know it, and that, limited though our understanding may be in this life, God is attempting to speak and eager that we should hear.

From the beginning, our Lord has been the divine Initiator in the process of the revelation of himself and of his ways to his beloved creation. By every rule of human logic, God should, perhaps, have turned his back on this little rebellious planet and left it to its own designs. But to the contrary, God has, from the beginning, been the pursuer. Man has been the pursued in God's relentless effort to declare his reality and his love.

The first revelation of God is from the heavens. There are so many stars that, though the psalmist said, "He calleth them all by their names," finite humans may never comprehend their magnitude. Had God arranged just a few stars to say, "I'm up here, and I love you," it would have been sufficient. But that is not the way of God. He is a gregarious, abundant, benevolent being who takes great delight in expressing his love beyond measure.

Why so many stars? Why the seeming excess of heavenly creation? The biblical reply is clear, "The heavens declare the glory of God, and the firmament sheweth his handiwork." The purpose of God's excessiveness is to arrest people's attention and create an aura in the natural order of things that will point people toward heaven.

God has further broadened the revelation of himself to the internal witness of human conscience. The earliest people possessed an innate quality intrensic in all human nature that makes them aware of some higher being to whom they are responsible and whom, in one fashion or another, they attempt to appease when doing wrong. Eve was troubled in her heart and questioned the temptor in Eden. The inner restraint of conscience made her think twice, and it was only with great uneasiness that she succumbed to the first temptation.

John said of Jesus, "That was the true Light, which lighteth every man that cometh into the world" (John 1:9). In the heart of every human being is a light. This light, this conscience, this God-consciousness, exists in all people. They do not know what the light is. They do not know that the vacuum is God-shaped, but all sense a need of something. They may attempt to fill it with idols of religion, sex, money, pleasure, fame, success, or a hundred other things, but they attempt to fill it with something. All of human creation is conditioned toward an awareness of God by the external witness of nature and the internal witness of the conscience.

Paul made this clear in Romans 1. He said there is enough of God revealed in nature that no one has an excuse before God in judgment relative to the internal response his heart makes to the external witness.

But these are only conditioning agents, and the continuing revelation of God is far more personal than these. He called Adam by name in the Garden. God spoke to Moses in the burning bush. He appeared to Abraham in a vision. In the wilderness, God guided the Hebrews with a cloud by day and a pillar of fire by night. Where they were, God led. Where they moved, Israel had to follow.

In the wilderness, God gave the tabernacle and its holy of holies as a personal representation of himself with precise accompanying directions for fellowship with him. The minutest details of the tabernacle, even to the colors of the curtains, spoke of God's revelation in Christ. Blue spoke of the heavens from whence he came; gold, of his diety; purple, of his royalty; and scarlet, of sacrifice.

When the people traveled, the tabernacle was folded, stored, and carried with meticulous precision. Still the people followed as the ark of the covenant led the procession, as the symbol of God's presence. Atop the ark was the mercy seat, the constant reminder that holy God would meet sinful people only at the point of innocent blood.

Within the ark of the covenant were the Law, reminder of obedience; the manna, picture of his provision; Aaron's rod which budded, reminder of the superiority of God's power—always the widening revelation of God to his people. Once inside the Promised Land, God's relationship to his people changed. He who would always condescend to meet humans at the point of their need would no longer be represented in a portable ark that moved. God chose to reveal his glory in the Temple of Solomon. Through the centuries, the prophets spoke, the kings reigned, and God was among his people.

During the centuries between the Old and New Testament eras, the Scriptures, though for the most part ignored, remained God's ultimate expression of himself to his people. Then our Lord Jesus Christ burst on the scene, introduced by the Baptist's immortal words, "Behold the Lamb of God, which taketh away the sin of the world" (John 1:29).

Now it was true, as the Hebrew writer would state, that

God, who at sundry times and in divers manners spake in time past unto the fathers by the prophets, Hath in these last days spoken unto us by his Son, whom he hath appointed heir of all things, by whom also he made the worlds; Who being the brightness of his glory, and the express image of his person, and upholding all things by the word of his power, when he had by himself purged our sins, sat down on the right hand of the Majesty on high; Being made so much better than the angels, as he hath by inheritance obtained a more excellent name than they (Heb. 1:1-4).

At the birth of Jesus, the angels sang, "Glory to God in the highest, and on earth peace, good will toward men." The first Christmas messenger heralded the message of God: "He shall be great, and shall be called the Son of the Highest: and the Lord God shall give unto him the throne of his father David: And he shall reign over the house of Jacob forever; and of his kingdom there shall be no end" (Luke 1:32-33).

At Jesus' baptism, the Spirit descended, and the Father spoke in joint confirmation of Trinitarian attestation, "This is my beloved Son, in whom I am well pleased." At the cross, the skies blackened, hell trembled, the rocks split, the graves opened, and the angels agonized in agreement with the centurion's testimony, "Truly this was the Son of God."

Please do not misunderstand what follows. For Jesus Christ is, indeed, the express image of the living God in whom "dwelleth all the fulness of the Godhead bodily." But while Jesus Christ is the full and complete revelation of the Father, his human incarnation for thirty-three years on earth was not the final revelation of the Father nor the Son to lost humanity. There were yet three other witnesses to come.

First, there is the witness of New Testament canon. "Search the Scriptures"; Christ said, "for in them ye think ye have eternal life: and they are they which testify of me." The Scriptures themselves, then, are a continuing witness of God to the world.

Secondly, the Holy Spirit continues to manifest the Father. While it is impossible to fully comprehend the mystery of the Trinity, suffice it to say that we would enhance our understanding if we were to refer to the Holy Spirit as the holy "Spirit of Christ," for he is precisely that—the invisible spiritual but literal presence of Jesus Christ among us. Once Jesus appeared in bodily form; now he is present in spiritual form. Invisible to the naked eye though he be, yet tangibly present, nonetheless. And so our Lord, beyond the physical and visible manifestation of himself in the Son, continues to speak through "the Spirit of his Son."

Thirdly, the "continuing incarnation" of Christ in his new body, the church, must certainly be understood as an essential revelation of the Father to all people. As believers in Christ, we comprise his body on earth fitly joined by the Spirit to the head in heaven. Now the world sees him no more, but they see him in us. We, as his people, become individually and collectively the tangible, visible expression of God to an unbelieving world.

"Father," Jesus said, "I pray ... that they all may be one ... that the world may believe that thou hast sent me." The harmony of the body of Christ loving, serving, functioning in the unity of the Spirit is a visible witness of the invisible God to a world that refuses to believe what it cannot see.

Jesus, who tabernacled himself in an earthly body for thirty-three years, now indwells the individual believer (Christ lives in you—you are the temple of the Holy Ghost). Above and beyond the individual incarnation is the perpetual incarnation of Christ in his entire body, the church, transcending generations and extending the revelation of her Lord to the world until he shall come personally in visible glory at the end of the tribulation.

Indeed, a mysterious and marvelous thought is that our Lord not only chose to reveal himself to mankind but also actually took the initiative and pursued a broadening course through history in the expression of that revelation. From the creation of the firmament to the rapture of his people, God has not left himself without a witness.

Wonderful though it is that God has gone to the extent to which the pursuit of his revelation has taken him, it is true that he has not fully revealed all to humanity. Much, therefore, must be categorized as mystery, for biblical record is clear that hidden in the councils of God are many truths we, in our natural state, may never know.

The prophet Isaiah made it clear that much has been hidden from us simply because we may not be trusted in our pride to know everything God knows.

I have declared the former things from the beginning; and they went forth out of my mouth, and I shewed them; I did them suddenly, and they came to pass. Because I knew that thou art obstinate, and thy neck is an iron sinew, and thy brow brass; I have even from the beginning declared it to thee; before it came to pass I shewed it thee; lest thou shouldest say, Mine idol hath done them, and my graven image, and my molten image, hath commanded them. Thou hast heard, see all this; and will not ye declare it? I have shewed thee new things from this time, even hidden things, and thou didst not know them. They are created now, and not from the beginning; even before the day when thou heardest them not; lest thou shouldest say, Behold, I knew them. Yea, thou heardest not; yea, thou knewest not; yea, from that time that thine ear was not opened: for I knew that thou wouldest deal very treacherously, and wast called a transgressor from the womb (Isa. 48:3-8).

Proud, sinful people may not, must not, and will not know all that God knows. God will reveal to us only as much as we may be trusted with. But God longs to reveal more than we know. One of the favorite Old Testament Scriptures is Jeremiah 33:3, "Call unto me, and I will answer thee, and shew thee great and mighty things, which thou knowest not." In the Hebrew language, "mighty things" should be interpreted "hidden things." God is saying that while it is true that we may not be trusted to know all things, he longs to give us insight into some things.

There are four degrees of God's things hidden from the minds of people. Four kinds of people in four states of understanding may be seen. Understand that the variables do not lie with the hidden things but with the kinds of people who are allowed broadening degrees of insight into the truth.

All Spiritual Things Are Hidden from the Lost Man

Unregenerate nature simply cannot comprehend spiritual truth. A Ph.D. in religion who is not born again knows less of the things of the Spirit than a ten-year-old who truly knows Christ. "The natural man receiveth not the things of the Spirit of God." The Bible gives three spiritual categories of humanity: the natural person in his lost, unregenerate state; the carnal person, saved by the Spirit, but controlled by the world and the flesh; and the spiritual person who is saved and controlled by the Spirit.

The natural person can hear the Word of God a thousand times, but to him it is foolish and irrelevant.

For the preaching of the cross is to them that perish foolishness; but unto us which are saved it is the power of God. For it is written, I will destroy the wisdom of the wise, and will bring to nothing the understanding of the prudent. Where is the wise? where is the scribe? where is the disputer of this world? hath not God made foolish the wisdom of this world? For after that in the wisdom of God the world by wisdom knew not God, it pleased God by the foolishness of preaching to save them that believe. For the Jews require a sign, and the Greeks seek after wisdom: But we preach Christ crucified, unto the Jews a stumblingblock, and unto the Greeks foolishness; But unto them which are called, both Jews and Greeks, Christ the power of God, and the wisdom of God. Because the foolishness of God is wiser than men; and the weakness of God is stronger than men. For ye see your calling, brethren, how that not many wise men after the flesh, not many mighty, not many noble, are called: but God hath chosen the foolish things of the world to confound the wise; and God hath chosen the weak things of the world to confound the things which are mighty; And base things of the world, and things which are despised, hath God chosen, yea, and things which are not, to bring to nought things that are (1 Cor. 1:18-28).

What a pity to see the unbeliever trying to understand problems that are spiritual in nature. Psychology has taken a turn toward "nondirective" counseling. The counselor begins with no fixed premises. The Bible has no relevancy, and to him there are no absolutes. He can, therefore, do little more than encourage the counselee to talk about himself. The psychologist does not recognize problems caused by sin nor understand the cure for guilt in the forgiveness of God.

The vast majority of persons with whom I have dealt who have gone for extensive counseling with unsaved psychiatrists have come out more confused than when they went in. To the humanist, Christianity is based on the preaching of a dead carpenter from Nazareth. It is absolutely ridiculous and totally irrelevant.

For that reason, simply declaring the gospel is not enough. We must pray the power of the Holy Spirit to ignite its dynamite into explosive force in the unbelieving heart.

The only understanding granted even the greatest of men is that which comes to those who would know Jesus in childlike faith.

Certain Mysteries Are Revealed Only to Believers

These mysteries lie in two categories. First are things that can be understood by faith and by experience. We may not understand fully the workings of substitutionary death and bodily resurrection, but we understand the concept. These things are not mysterious to believers. They have a grasp of these concepts, an understanding. Believers understand the hope of eternal life that resides in the soul. They are cognizant of the witness of the Spirit and can respond to his leadings. Believers understand that we gain by losing and live by dying. They may not fully understand the peace of God, but they know what they experience in the "peace ..., which passeth all understanding."

The second type of understanding believers have is the special insight given when the Spirit reveals spiritual truth to human understanding. Believers may read a Scripture passage a thousand times, but then really see it for the first time. What they have believed mentally dawns upon them spiritually and experientially. God has illuminated his Word, applied his truth, and given the "witness of the Spirit." For years I have taught the same Bible study every Tuesday and Wednesday three different times to three different groups in a space of thirty hours. Each time I teach the Bible study a little different way, for each time I receive additional insight. The second is better than the first and the third superior to the second. I wonder sometimes how much insight the Lord could continue to give on the same passage were I to teach it one hundred times in a row.

One Category of Spiritual Things Even the Believer Cannot Understand

The natural person can understand no spiritual truths; the carnal person understands only enough truth to accept salvation. The spiritual person understands the basics and progressively gets insight into deeper understanding. But there is still much that even the mature believer cannot fully comprehend.

I believe Romans 8:28, but I do not fully comprehend it. I cannot explain how it is that the more I give the more I have, but I have experienced it and I know that it works. I cannot comprehend the incarnation, though I believe it. How is it that the lesser can contain the greater, that God could become a man? How is it that Jesus is the Son of God and yet God himself? How could he pray to the Father and yet say, "He that hath seen me hath seen the Father." The incarnation is a mystery; the Trinity is a mystery. We can believe them, but we cannot explain them.

Fullness of Understanding Is Reserved for the Glorification of the Believer in Heaven

Regardless of how much we may know in this life, we will never know all things. Conversely, it is true that regardless of how little we may know here, we shall one day have perfect knowledge. We may only learn 1, 10, or 90 percent of the deep, hidden things of God. But at glorification, and that in itself is one of our great mysteries, we shall know all things.

All mystery will finally be revealed to the "man in Christ." The mystery will not be changed. It has been an understandable, knowledgeable entity all the time. Our capacity to "know" will be changed. For then we shall know as we are known and all understanding will be ours.

But our Lord would not have us wait until then to broaden our understanding. Regardless of how little we know, we may and we must know more. He is pleased when we desire to know, and he desires that we know more than we do. He is the willing Revelator of himself to all who long for him and who believe his earnest promise, "seek, and ye shall find."

2
The Mystery of
the Kingdom

And the disciples came, and said unto him, Why speakest thou unto them in parables? He answered and said unto them, Because it is given unto you to know the mysteries of the kingdom of heaven, but to them it is not given. For whosoever hath, to him shall be given, and he shall have more abundance: but whosoever hath not, from him shall be taken away even that he hath. Therefore speak I to them in parables: because they seeing see not; and hearing they hear not, neither do they understand. And in them is fulfilled the prophecy of Esaias, which saith, By hearing ye shall hear, and shall not understand; and seeing ye shall see, and shall not perceive: For this people's heart is waxed gross, and their ears are dull of hearing, and their eyes they have closed; lest at any time they should see with their eyes, and hear with their ears, and should understand with their heart, and should be converted, and I should heal them. But blessed are your eyes, for they see: and your ears, for they hear. For verily I say unto you, That many prophets and righteous men have desired to see those things which ye see, and have not seen them; and to hear those things which ye hear and have not heard them. Hear ye therefore the parable of the sower (Matt. 13:10-18).

Jesus made it clear that the kingdom of God is a mystery. More than merely a mystery, it is one of the greatest mysteries of the Bible. While it is perhaps the most difficult of the mysteries for the world, it may well be the one into which the believer may gain the most insight.

The Scriptures are replete with analogies which picture the relationship of Christ and his own. He is the Groom; we are the bride. He is the Foundation; we, the building. He is the Vine, and we the branches. He is the Shepherd, and we, the sheep. No more picturesque or meaningful illustration is to be seen, though, than that of a loving King graciously ruling over willing subjects.

The kingdom of God presupposes a King, subjects, and a constitution, or principles by which the kingdom operates. Let us look first at the kingdom itself. There is much speculation as to whether the expression "the kingdom of heaven" and "the kingdom of God" are, in fact, two names for the same thing. While it is likely that the two may, in fact, be one, the possibility of two separate concepts might be understood in terms of that which is now and that which was before and will be after.

In the Model Prayer, our Lord taught us to pray, "Thy kingdom come, Thy will be done in earth, as it is in heaven." From the Greek, the meaning is clear. The desire of our Lord is that the kingdom of heaven come on earth and that the will of God be done on earth. In heaven, the will of God is always done. It is a place where willing subjects gladly accept the rule of King Jesus. The only rebellion against that authority has long since been put down and the integrity of the kingdom nature maintained.

One day during the millennial reign of Christ on earth the kingdom of heaven will also be established on this planet. Then, as it is now in heaven, the will of God under the rule of King Jesus will again be done. The kingdom of heaven, then, refers to a place, a condition, a life-style in which every subject gladly honors and serves the King. That happened before time began, is happening now in heaven, and will happen on earth during the millennium. It will continue to happen throughout eternity under the rule of King Jesus.

There is, however, one glaring exception to the willing rule of the citizens of the eternal universe under the King. This earth is under the control of worldly, godless, rebellious humanity and under the dominion of satanic power. The name of the game on planet Earth is rebellion against the King. This world and its powers have no intention of bowing before his lordship. However, the time will come when such will not be the case. For when Christ returns in judgment over the nations of the world, "Every knee should bow, ... and that every tongue should confess Jesus Christ is Lord, to the glory of God the Father."

Where, then, on this rebellious planet may the kingdom be found? Our Lord's answer to that question is that the kingdom of God is within us. Though there is no worldwide peace on this rebellious planet, some individuals are walking islands of peace because they are willing subjects of the King.

At conversion, Christ is enthroned on the heart of

the penitent believer as Lord and King. Here he rules in complete accord with the desire of the heart that has come to love and honor him as King.

If there is, then, a difference in the expressions "kingdom of God" and "kingdom of heaven," the kingdom of heaven may be a condition in which all inhabitants of a particular era of time are subjects to the rule of him whose will is done as it is in heaven. The kingdom of God may be defined as the rule of the King in the heart of an individual who inhabits a kingdom under the control of the evil one. The kingdom of God is within you.

The kingdom of heaven must have a king. If a kingdom presupposes subjects willingly ruled, it also includes a king. One entire Gospel was written to say that Jesus alone is the King. Matthew was written with Jews in mind. More references were made to Christ as King by Matthew than by the other three Gospel writers combined.

Jesus, the Messiah, had to come through the lineage of Israel's most powerful leader, King David. In no uncertain terms, Matthew set him forth, not only as David's descendant but also as David's King. The greatest of Jewish kings is "KING OF KINGS, AND LORD OF LORDS."

Someone has said, "He is not King by man's decree. You may acknowledge Him as King or attempt to deny His kingship, but He is King anyhow." Jesus is pictured in Revelation as returning on a white horse in splendor and glory, bringing judgment to the systems of a rebellious world: "He hath on his vesture and on his thigh a name written, King of kings, and Lord of lords."

Were Charlemagne and Napoleon, Washington and Lincoln, Plato and Aristotle to walk into a room together, we should all stand to honor them. But were Jesus Christ to enter the room, we would fall upon our faces and worship him. Jesus Christ is King! Hallelujah!!

Further, a kingdom presupposes a constitution, embodying the purpose and principles upon which the kingdom stands. The constitution to the kingdom of heaven is recorded in Matthew 5, 6, and 7. These chapters record the purpose of life, the nature of being, the recipe for fulfillment, and the relationship to the King which makes possible the reality of the kingdom.

As with all such documents, there is a beautiful preamble. It sums up the purpose of its existence. One theme is stated repeatedly.

Blessed are the poor in spirit: for theirs is the kingdom of heaven. Blessed are they that mourn: for they shall be comforted. Blessed are the meek: for they shall inherit the earth. Blessed are they which do hunger and thirst after righteousness: for they shall be filled. Blessed are the merciful: for they shall obtain mercy. Blessed are the pure in heart: for they shall see God. Blessed are the peacemakers: for they shall be called the children of God. Blessed are they which are persecuted for righteousness' sake: for theirs is the kingdom of heaven. Blessed are ye, when men shall revile you, and persecute you, and shall say all manner of evil against you falsely, for my sake. Rejoice, and be exceeding glad: for great is your reward in heaven: for so persecuted they the prophets which were before you (Matt. 5:3-12).

Nine times the theme word *blessed* is repeated. What does this word mean? It means "happy." Listen to it. Think it through. Read it again. Let it grip you. The purpose of the kingdom is the happiness of its subjects.

King Jesus came to make people happy, and the constitution tells us what true happiness is. In a simple sentence, happiness is the right relationship to the King. But it is a fellowship with one who not only rules over you but also lives within you and gives you the power to live according to his precepts.

Who was the happiest, most well-adjusted and fulfilled person who ever lived? None other than our King himself, the Lord Jesus. Despised? Rejected? Forsaken? Impoverished? None of these ruffled him. External conditions were of little importance. Individuals may experience internal happiness and complete joy within when Christ is seated on the throne of the believer's heart. Regardless of what the world says or does, the reigning King within may give happiness to the willing subject always and in all ways.

Let us return to Matthew 13:18, where our Lord taught of the mystery of the kingdom of heaven. You will recall that in verses 10 and 11, Jesus spoke in parables because it is not given to the unbeliever to understand the mysteries of the kingdom of heaven. Notice that Jesus used the word *mysteries*. The plural is definitely intended to convey that there are several concepts about the kingdom of heaven which the believer must understand, but which are locked to the unbeliever, if he is to comprehend the kingdom of heaven.

The key to unlocking the mysteries of the kingdom, then, is finding the pivotal word for the whole chapter. It is the word "therefore" contained in verse 18. In review, our Lord said that the kingdom of heaven is a mystery, it is many mysteries, it may not be comprehended by the world, and it is spoken in parables. "Therefore," hear the parable of the sower (v. 18). The secret of understanding the mystery of the kingdom, then, is understanding the parables.

In this context, our Lord taught seven parables containing six principles which unlock the mystery of the kingdom. Let us attempt to unlock them with the key of the understanding of the Spirit. There are approximately thirty-two parables which illustrate the essence of the six main principles of the kingdom contained in these six specific parables.

Don't Judge the Kingdom by Its Subjects— The Parable of the Sower

And he spake many things unto them in parables, saying, Behold, a sower went forth to sow; And when he sowed, some seeds fell by the way side, and the fowls came and devoured them up: Some fell upon stony places, where they had no much earth: and forthwith they sprung up, because they had no deepness of earth: And when the sun was up, they were scorched; and because they had no root, they withered away. And some fell among thorns; and the thorns sprung up, and choked them: But other fell into good ground, and brought forth fruit, some an hundredfold, some sixtyfold, some thirtyfold. . . . Hear ye therefore the parable of the sower. When any one heareth the word of the kingdom, and understandeth it not, then cometh the wicked one, and catcheth away that which was sown in his heart. This is he which received seed by the way side. But he that received the seed into stony places, the same is he that heareth the word, and anon with joy receiveth it; Yet hath he not root in himself, but dureth for a while: for when tribulation or persecution ariseth because of the word, by and by he is offended. He also that received seed among the thorns is he that heareth the word; and the care of this world, and the deceitfulness of riches, choke the word, and he becometh unfruitful. But he that received seed into the good ground is he that heareth the word, and understandeth it; which also beareth fruit, and bringeth forth, some an hundredfold, some sixty, some thirty (Matt. 13:3-8,18-23).

The first principle of the kingdom locked in this parable is don't judge the kingdom by its subjects. In the story of the sower, the earth is the heart, the Lord is the sower, the devil is the enemy.

In every congregation some people hear the Word and immediately respond. The ground is shallow, the heart has not been adequately prepared, and the commitment is thin. No sooner will the sun of adversity and temptation arise than the faith of the pseudobeliever will fail. In the heart of some, the preparation has been more thorough and the commitment more genuine. Though they do not fail as quickly, they, too, will eventually allow the thorns of evil to choke the beauty of the Word. But there are those people whose hearts are genuinely ready, whose commitments are eternal, and whose lives, fruitful. Those people are true Christians, for it is the nature of saving faith that it endures. It does not become saving faith by enduring, but its very endurance validates the reality of its nature.

The point of the parable is simple. The Word does not change. The Word is powerful, effective, and well able to save to the uttermost. The change occurs within the heart. The variance in the parable is not the efficacy of the Word but the response of the hearer.

How often do we hear, "I knew a man once who made a profession of faith, followed Christ a few months, and quit. Surely there is nothing in Christianity for me." Conversely it is true, however, that we know hundreds who have professed their faith in Christ only to follow him for decades, even unto death. Unfortunately, the world too often fails to recognize them. But the truth is that neither are to be the standard by which the kingdom is to be judged.

Men come and go, but the Word does not change. Though men fail, God's Word cannot. The fairest saint that you may know will one day fail and disappoint you in some way. Young Christian, keep your eyes on the Lord Jesus Christ. He is the living Word, and he, and he alone, will not fail you. Don't judge the kingdom by its subjects.

Don't Judge the Kingdom on a Short-Sighted Basis— The Parable of the Wheat and Tares

Another parable put he forth unto them, saying, The kingdom of heaven is likened unto a man which sowed good seed in his field; But while men slept, his enemy came and sowed tares among the wheat, and went his way. But when the blade was sprung up, and brought forth fruit, then appeared the tares also. So the servants of the householder came and said unto him, Sir, didst not thou sow good seed in thy field? from whence then hath it tares? He said unto them, An enemy hath done this. The servants said unto him, Wilt thou then that we go and gather them up? But he said, Nay; lest while ye gather up the tares, ye root up also the wheat with them. Let both grow together until the harvest: and in the

time of harvest I will say to the reapers, Gather ye together
first the tares, and bind them in bundles to burn them: but
gather the wheat into my barn (Matt. 13:24-30).

Far too often harm is done in the church by as-
suming that that which appears to be wheat is wheat
and that which appears to be tares is tares. The point
of this parable is that time will tell. We must not be
premature in our judgments. Jesus said, "Let both
grow together until the harvest" (v. 30).

What appears to be weeds may only be the seri-
ous struggle of a young convert. The fledgling Christian has a long way to go and has to be nurtured and
encouraged, rather than condemned. On the other
hand, some who appear to be strong wheat may, in
fact, be hypocrites.

How are we to tell? That is not our job. We are not
to spend our lives judging other people. That is the
business of the Judge alone and may well be left to the
inerrant discernment of the King. Often we are reminded that weak and sinful people attend our
churches. But let it be remembered that the church is
not a showcase for the saints but a hospital for sinners.

In attempting to set ourselves up as spiritual
judges, we will often do more harm than good by mistakenly rooting out some wheat with the tares (v. 29).
Our King, as the only perfect Judge, is well able to
handle this delicate issue. The key word of the parable
is "until" (v. 30). "Let both grow together until the
harvest." The Lord's time of reaping, separation,
judgment, punishment, and reward is not yet. We
make a mistake if we hurry in our judgments. Time
will tell. Let the King judge the subjects. Let God be
God. Don't judge the kingdom on a shortsighted basis.

Don't Underestimate the Power and Potential of the Kingdom— The Parable of the Mustard Seed

Another parable put he forth unto them, saying, The kingdom of heaven is like to a grain of mustard seed, which a man took, and sowed in his field: Which indeed is the least of all seeds: but when it is grown, it is the greatest among herbs, and becometh a tree, so that the birds of the air come and lodge in the branches thereof (Matt. 13:31-32).

The mustard seed is the tiniest of seeds. The watermelon seed may call it insignificant. The avacado seed may look contemptuously upon it. But though it appears by men to be insignificant, it has the potential of great power and influence.

In the eyes of the world the kingdom of God is nothing. It is less than nothing. The church and the cause of Jesus Christ are, to an unbelieving society, simply not a force to be reckoned with. Science is the thing; education is king; wealth is god; power is all that matters. The church is insignificant, irrelevant, despised—nothing. But one man who turns his cheek, one young woman who stands alone, one church that dares to dream can touch a society and change a world.

You err if you despise the power of the kingdom because of the comparative smallness of its numbers. The church is never strongest when it is the biggest. Her power may not be measured in her numerical strength. Don't underestimate the church. Don't underestimate the kingdom.

Don't Underestimate the Potential of the Kingdom— The Parable of the Leaven

"Another parable spake he unto them; The kingdom of heaven is like unto leaven, which a woman took, and hid in three measures of meal, till the whole was leavened" (Matt. 13:33). The kingdom of God at work in the world through the internal ministry of the King in human hearts has within it the potential to bring heaven on earth. Leaven doesn't make any noise. It has no odor and little substance. But slowly and surely its presence is felt, its force expands to the bursting point.

There is no question that Bible prophecy is clear. The Lord of the kingdom will never make the earth change for good. Evil, unfortunately, will win out temporarily until Christ comes and sets up his kingdom. But understand clearly the whole world could change if people would only allow it the opportunity to do so.

Every problem in society could be solved. Every need met, every rebellion ceased, every inequity satisfied, every marriage saved, every jail emptied if the kingdom were allowed to have its way. Everything the world is looking for may be found, not in politics and education, not in sin, philosophy, and international military aggression, but in the kingdom of heaven.

Getting into the Kingdom Is Worth the Price— The Parables of the Hidden Treasure and the Pearl Merchant

Again, the kingdom of heaven is like unto treasure hid in a field; the which when a man hath found, he hideth, and for joy thereof goeth and selleth all that he hath, and buyeth that field. Again, the kingdom of heaven is like unto a merchant man, seeking goodly pearls: Who, when he had found one pearl of great price, went and sold all that he had and bought it (Matt. 13:44-46).

There must be no question that there is a cost to enter the kingdom of heaven. The price has been paid by Christ on the cross, but the cost is yours to pay.

Often I am asked, "How much will it cost me to join your church?" The only answer I know to give is, "Everything you have." Our Lord will settle for nothing less than total commitment. To the rich young ruler, the cost was his earthly possessions; to the man tied to the family apron strings, it was forsake your mother and father and "follow me"; to the fisherman by the seaside it was leaving their boats and business; to the tax collector, it was leaving his position; to the worldly woman, it was "go, and sin no more"; to the timid, it was "confess me before men."

Yes, there is a cost for following Christ. But this important mystery of the kingdom states simply that whatever the cost, the gain is worth the sacrifice.

"Whosoever Will May Come"— The Parable of the Net

Again, the kingdom of heaven is like unto a net, that was cast into the sea, and gathered of every kind: Which, when it was full, they drew to shore, and sat down, and gathered the good into vessels, but cast the bad away. So shall it be at the end of the world: the angels shall come forth, and sever the wicked from among the just, And shall cast them into the furnace of fire: there shall be wailing and gnashing of teeth (Matt. 13:47-50).

Many secondary truths are to be found in this parable. It includes the fact that the King has it all in control and in his good time will make the final determination between the saved and the lost. It contains the truth that there is eternal destruction for the unrighteous and endless torment in the lake of fire. It teaches, as did the parable of the wheat and tares, that God alone is the able discerner of the hearts.

But the primary teaching of this parable is that one of the great mysteries of the kingdom lies in its universal appeal and the resultant complexity of its citizenship. What a glorious sight it will be in heaven to see the procession gathered by the angels from the four corners of the earth. From East and West they come: the rich and the poor; the healthy and the infirmed; the black, the white, the yellow and brown. From every walk of life and every tongue will be a multitude that no one can number. Is there any question that there is no greater international or domestic issue than the ability of the different peoples of the world's nations to get along with each other. The heart cry of the human race is for peace. But peace with others is only possible as a result of peace with God. No sociological structure, no political decree, no sectarian human organization will ever bind the hearts of people together on this earth.

A kingdom is coming whose law is love and whose cohesive dimension lies in the binding nature of mutual love for the King which gives his willing subjects love for each other. Possible on earth? It is possible but only in the kingdom of heaven under the rule of King Jesus.

3
The Mystery of
the Gospel

Praying always with all prayer and supplication in the Spirit, and watching thereunto with all perseverance and supplication for all saints; And for me, that utterance may be given unto me, that I may open my mouth boldly, to make known the mystery of the gospel, For which I am an ambassador in bonds: that therein I may speak boldly, as I ought to speak (Eph. 6:18-20).

Paul was an ambassador for Christ, a messenger commissioned by the King to declare his Word in its fullness. Of all the words Paul loved most, he appears to have an unusual affinity for the term *the gospel.* He loved it, preached it, taught it, defended it, and was absolutely unashamed to live and die for its purity and proclamation. If heaven shall reveal that our risen Lord spoke more to Paul than is recorded in the account of his conversion, it is quite possible that a personal recitation of the Great Commission to "preach the gospel to every creature" was included. This alone, perhaps, could account for the burning heat of the missionary's heart which flung him onto foreign fields as a servant and martyr of Christ whose gospel Paul proclaimed.

The gospel was important to Paul. He was unashamed of it and proclaimed it to a pseudointellectual society whose Jewish and Gentile members alike scoffed with scorn at the message of a carpenter crucified on the city garbage dump of Jerusalem.

But Paul's message was more than a message of a cross. The resurrection and his personal experience with the resurrected One gave dynamism to his ministry. Paul made it absolutely clear the gospel to him included the resurrection of Jesus, as well as his death.

Moreover, brethren, I declare unto you the gospel which I preached unto you, which also ye have received, and wherein ye stand; By which also ye are saved, if ye keep in memory what I preached unto you, unless ye have believed in vain. For I delivered unto you first of all that which I also received, how that Christ died for our sins according to the scriptures; And that he was buried, and that he rose again the third day according to the scriptures: And that he was seen of Cephas, then of the twelve: After that, he was seen of above five hundred brethren at once; of whom the greater part remain unto this present, but some are fallen asleep. After that, he was seen of James; then of all the apostles. And last of all he was seen of me also, as of one born out of due time (1 Cor. 15:1-8).

This humble Jewish evangelist had no doubts that Christ had risen from the dead. Had he not, after all, appeared to "me also" (v. 8)? Further, Christ's grace allowed so complete a turnaround that he who once persecuted the church now defended it. Paul said he could do nothing else than that which grace constrained and compelled, "Woe is unto me, if I preach not the gospel."

In the closing words of the letter to the Ephesian church (6:18-20), Paul pled with the believers to intercede with their Lord in his behalf, "that utterance may be given unto me, ... to make known the mystery of the gospel" (v. 19).

The Word of God is at once *Logos* and *Rhema* to the believer. The changeless and fixed revelation of the Scriptures must be made *Rhema*, or personal, to each who hears. Far from this is the profession of some charismatics that everyone may believe what he wants about the Scriptures. That is not what Paul intended. No Scripture passage is open to private interpretation. The Scriptures do not simply mean what it means to you. It means what it means whether you exist or not. But the *Rhema*—the Word made personal—means that the Bible has specific and unique application to the need of your personal life at the particular time you hear it!!

Paul's great prayer was that God would use him as an articulate instrument to unfold the mystery of God's good news in Christ in such a way as to be "all things to all men" that he "might by all means save some." Paul did not pray for a new revelation of truth for each occasion, for he said, if "we, or an angel from heaven, preach any other gospel unto you than that which we have preached unto you, let him be accursed" (Gal. 1:8).

Paul's request to the Ephesian church was for prayer in his behalf to be sensitive and understanding to the needs of the human heart and unlocking the

truth of the gospel, as they pertain to all who heard
him on any particular given occasion. This is what
every sincere minister longs for. Every devout church
member should aptly commit himself to the prayerful
support of his pastor in the study and presentation of
gospel truth.

The word *gospel* means good news. The four Gospels present the good news of the ministry and teachings of the life of Jesus Christ. Jesus incarnated the
good news. The dynamite of its explosive force mod-
eled, each day of the Savior's earthly ministry, the
truth that he spoke. The gospel is a two-edged sword,
at once bearing judgment to break the icy crags of evil
in the human heart and the sunshine of love to melt it
into a sweet river of peace. It is, indeed, "grace that
taught my heart to fear, And grace my fears relieved."

We mistakenly refer to the first four books of the
New Testament as the four Gospels. They are, rather,
one gospel recorded by four men. Jesus did and said
much that was profound. It was impossible for one
man to adequately record it all. Today, a presidential
candidate has hundreds of reporters on his trail, recording every word. In just such a way, several reporters were required to put together one gospel in
four books to allow a complete composite of the life and
teachings of Jesus Christ. Even at this, John spoke
well when he said, "There are also many other things
which Jesus did, ... I suppose that even the world
itself could not contain the books that should be written" (John 21:25).

But much more must be understood to fully
comprehend the purpose of four accounts of the gospel. Matthew, Mark, Luke, and John's perspectives

were different. Each wrote from a different back-
ground and to a different segment of society. The purpose in writing each account, therefore, was to con-
vince that segment that Jesus Christ was for them.
Combined, then, the one gospel presented by four
authors says, "Jesus Christ is for everybody."

Matthew's account was strictly for the Jews.
Matthew, the tax collector, was concerned with specific details. He made his living recording incomes,
family trees, relatives, and histories. He wanted the
Jews to know specifically that King Jesus was at once
the descendant of, and greater than, not only King
David but the founder of Judaism, Abraham, as well.

In Matthew's first chapter, he traced the genealogy of the Lord Jesus to Abraham. As Abraham's
Lord, "Before Abraham was, I am" and as David's
king, Jesus was both the descendant of and before
Abraham and David. Twenty-seven of Matthew's
twenty-eight chapters refer to Jesus as King. Matthew recorded that above the cross of Jesus was an
inscription, "THIS IS JESUS THE KING OF THE
JEWS."

Matthew used more Old Testament Scriptures
than the other three gospel writers combined. Matthew's message is that the Christ had come precisely
as was necessary to be King of the Jews.

Mark's Gospel was written to the Romans. Mark
understood the servant mind-set. The Roman empire
was built upon a slave culture. Sixty million slaves did
the bidding of the emperor. They were uninterested
and unimpressed with royal chronologies. Mark wrote
no genealogy.

Mark wanted the Romans to know that he was a

willing bond servant to the Lord Jesus who was, in turn, a love slave to the Father. In effect, Mark said, "Listen, you Romans, Jesus Christ is like you are. He worked, he sweat, he suffered, he was lonely, he hurt, he died an agonizing death, he relates to you, he identifies with you, he understands you. He is, therefore, well aware of the servant-master relationship. By making him your Master, you can know the joy and freedom that he knew in willing servitude and obedience to his Father."

The Romans were a people of suffering and death. They were a people of the earth, so he wrote about geography. They were an irreligious people, so Mark made only two references to the Old Testament. The Romans did not know the Old Testament. They were disinterested and uninformed. To be sure, there are more than two quotations from the Old Testament in his account, but he was merely quoting Jesus who quoted the Scriptures. Mark's only two additions are a quotation from Malachi and one from Isaiah. He was not writing to Jews, he was writing to Roman servants.

Luke was a physician, and as such, was interested in the human issues of birth, life, and death. The Greeks were humanists, and Luke wrote to them. In Luke's genealogy, he traced the Lord Jesus back to Adam, the first man (Luke 3:38). The message of Luke is that Jesus Christ is not just for the Jews, but for everybody. Jesus Christ is for the whole human race.

In Luke, the prodigal represents all wayward humanity returning to the Father. In Luke, the good Samaritan pictures people from all walks of life. Doctor

Luke's purpose was to show the universal appeal of the gospel of our Lord.

John, the philosopher theologian, traced the Lord Jesus all the way back to God. The predominant religious philosophy of John's day was gnosticism. In part, this never ending strain of religious philosophical thought, taught that a holy God could never condescend to touch unholy human flesh. Jesus Christ, then, could not be God, for he possessed a physical body.

John's great theme was "the Word was made flesh." In his epistles, John said that we have handled him, touched him, and "seen [him] with our eyes." For whom was John writing? John's Gospel was for the church. It was to the believer that he appealed. The faith of fledgling Christians in a belligerent society had to be supported. "Take heart—Jesus Christ is God."

John, himself, was exiled as a political criminal for his own unyieldingness to the Roman confession, "Caesar is Lord."

"No," John said, "Jesus Christ is Lord." "For the word of God, and for the testimony of Jesus Christ" John was exiled in the Aegean Sea (Rev. 1:9).

Christ's deity and his incarnation are John's favorite themes. To the believer the message is: Take hope. What you have believed and that wherein you stand is right. Jesus Christ is the eternal transcendent, incarnate Son of God superseding all denominations of time and space.

I am that bread of life.... Then spake Jesus again unto them, saying, I am the light of the world: he that followeth me shall not walk in darkness, but shall have the light of life.... Jesus said unto them, Verily, verily, I say unto you, Before Abraham was, I am.... I am the door: by me if any man enter in, he shall be saved, and shall go in and out, and find pasture.... I am the good shepherd: the good shepherd giveth his life for the sheep.... Jesus saith unto him, I am the way, the truth, and the life: no man cometh unto the Father, but by me.... I am the true vine, and my Father is the husbandman (John 6:48; 8:12,58; 10:9,11; 14:6; 15:1).

The mystery of the gospel reaches far beyond the dimensions of philosophical and theological thought. For "the faith which was once delivered unto the saints" is good news for a lost humanity that desperately needs something to cheer about. It is, indeed, "out of the ivory palaces" that Jesus came, but he stepped into the cesspool of society and the garbage heap of humanity.

The mystery of the gospel, then, must be understood not merely in terms of philosophy but in terms of spiritual poverty. To the man on the street, the apostle Paul made practical and relevant the truth of John's transcended theology. The world needs to hear of this good news. Its simple message is threefold:

The Mystery of the Humility of the Gospel

Jesus Christ was not born in a palace, but in a manger. He slept not in brass beds, but barren caves. "The Son of man hath not where to lay his head." He worked miracles to provide food for his listeners and went to the mouth of a fish to afford the price of Roman taxation. He was born in a borrowed stable, rode on a borrowed donkey, and was buried in a borrowed tomb. The only thing that was his own was his cross.

This very character of humility may be that which causes so many to stumble.

For the preaching of the cross is to them that perish foolishness; but unto us which are saved it is the power of God. For it is written, I will destroy the wisdom of the wise, and will bring to nothing the understanding of the prudent. Where is the wise? where is the scribe? where is the disputer of this world? hath not God made foolish the wisdom of this world? For after that in the wisdom of God the world by wisdom knew not God, it pleased God by the foolishness of preaching to save them that believe. For the Jews require a sign, and the Greeks seek after wisdom: But we preach Christ crucified, unto the Jews a stumblingblock, and unto the Greeks foolishness; But unto them which are called, both Jews and Greeks, Christ the power of God, and the wisdom of God. Because the foolishness of God is wiser than men; and the weakness of God is stronger than men. For ye see your calling, brethren, how that not many wise men after the flesh, not many mighty, not many noble, are called: But God hath chosen the foolish things of the world to confound the wise; and God hath chosen the weak things of the world to confound the things which are mighty; And base things of the world, and things which are despised, hath God chosen, yea, and things which are not, to bring to nought things that are: That no flesh should glory in his presence. But of him are ye in Christ Jesus, who of God is made unto us wisdom, and righteousness, and sanctification, and redemption: That, according as it is written, He that glorieth, let him glory in the Lord (1 Cor. 1:18-31).

At the basis of every false religion is the effort of human goodness. "Do something" cries everything within us. No clearer dividing line between truth and error may be seen than that to which religious and philosophical thought may be boiled down, *Is man jus-*

tified by grace through faith or by the works of the flesh? "For by grace are ye saved through faith; and that not of yourselves: it is the gift of God: Not of works, lest any man should boast. For we are his workmanship, created in Christ Jesus unto good works, which God hath before ordained that we should walk in them" (Eph. 2:8-10). "To declare, I say, at this time his righteousness: that he might be just, and the justifier of him which believeth in Jesus. Where is boasting then? It is excluded. By what law? of works? Nay: but by the law of faith. Therefore we conclude that a man is justified by faith without the deeds of the law" (Rom. 3:26-28).

Every new religion that comes along gets its share of devotees. Intrinsic in human nature is the universal and satanic tendency to exalt the self.

How art thou fallen from heaven, O Lucifer, son of the morning! how art thou cut down to the ground, which didst weaken the nations! For thou hast said in thine heart, I will ascend into heaven, I will exalt my throne above the stars of God: I will sit also upon the mount of the congregation, in the sides of the north: I will ascend above the heights of the clouds; I will be like the most High (Isa. 14:12-14).

Our Lord was not crucified in a royal palace between kings, but on the city garbage dump between two thieves. He died at the crossroads of the world, identifying himself with sinful, depraved humanity where he who had known no sin became sin for us. It is still "the way of the cross" that leads home. The way up is down.

Just as I am, without one plea,
But that thy blood was shed for me,
And that thou bidd'st me come to thee,
O Lamb of God, I come! I come!

The Mystery of Its Universality

The Jews were confounded that the Lord Jesus would offer salvation to the Gentiles, as well as to them. We often refer to the Jewish people as the chosen people. But chosen to do what? Simply this: They were chosen to be the agency through which the gospel would come to the world. But when they refused to receive their own Messiah, the privilege of being God's people was given to the Gentiles. It is, therefore, "whosoever will" may come. "For God so loved the world." Isaiah's plaintive plea, "Ho every one that thirsteth, come ye to the waters," now has universal meaning.

In the opening words of Ephesians, Paul wrote of this unspeakable wonder:

That in the dispensation of the fulness of times he might gather together in one all things in Christ, both which are in heaven, and which are on earth; even in him: In whom also we have obtained an inheritance, being predestinated according to the purpose of him who worketh all things after the counsel of his own will: That we should be to the praise of his glory, who first trusted in Christ (Eph. 1:10-12).

The Simplicity of the Gospel.

To the Jews, ceremony was all-important, and everything required a sign. To the proud Greeks, self-righteousness was the only thing. By their own good works and pride, they sought to achieve salvation. In the Gentile world, knowledge was god. Intellect was everything and salvation to both for but a privileged few.

The simplicity of the gospel for all men, then, was a staggering thing. That by faith—not visible signs, by repentance of self-righteous—not the work of human effort, man was to be justified before God was unbelievable. NEVER! But this very simplicity is a great part of the mystery of the gospel.

Who can forget the appeal of the humble servants to their powerful master, General Naaman, who refused to submit to the humiliation of cleansing? "If the prophet had bid thee do some great thing, wouldest thou not have done it?" And it is to the Naaman's of this world—the elite, the affluent, the religious, the educated, the great—that Paul's words still speak:

For Christ sent me not to baptize, but to preach the gospel: not with wisdom of words, lest the cross of Christ should be made of none effect. For the preaching of the cross is to them that perish foolishness; but unto us which are saved it is the power of God. For it is written, I will destroy the wisdom of the wise, and will bring to nothing the understanding of the prudent (1 Cor. 1:17-19).

In 1957, Billy Graham preached for three months in London. As he was boarding the plane to fly back to America, a reporter said to him, "Mr. Graham, you have set religion back in this country fifty years."

The humble evangelist replied, "Then I have failed, sir, for I meant to set it back two thousand years."

The humble, universal, simple, and eternal import of the mystery of the gospel message is still in its death and resurrection message, its cleansing blood, and its powerful salvation on the basis of repentance and faith. In the words of Katherine Hankey:

> I love to tell the story Of unseen things above,
> Of Jesus and His glory, Of Jesus and His love:
> I love to tell the story Because I know 'tis true;
> It satisfies my longings As nothing else can do.
> I love to tell the story, 'Twill be my theme in glory
> To tell the old, old story of Jesus and His love.

4
The Mystery of
the Church

Husbands, love your wives, even as Christ also loved the church, and gave himself for it; That he might sanctify and cleanse it with the washing of water by the word, That he might present it to himself a glorious church, not having spot, or wrinkle, or any such thing; but that it should be holy and without blemish. So ought men to love their wives as their own bodies. He that loveth his wife loveth himself. For no man ever yet hated his own flesh; but nourisheth and cherisheth it, even as the Lord the church: For we are members of his body, of his flesh, and of his bones. For this cause shall a man leave his father and mother, and shall be joined unto his wife, and they two shall be one flesh. This is a great mystery: but I speak concerning Christ and the church (Eph. 5:25-32).

The Genius of the Church: Its Mystical Union with Christ

In the above passage the apostle Paul taught that the relationship of a man to his bride is the same as the relationship of Christ, the beloved husband to whom we are espoused, and his bride, the church. Let it be understood at the outset that the word *church* does not refer to an ecclesiastical denomination or a building of bricks and mortar. The church of the New Testament is presented in two ways.

First, it exists as the true church, the corporate body of Christ on earth. Secondly, the New Testament word *church* refers 90 percent of the time to a local body of believers, functioning as a tangible, physical witness of Christ to their particular geographical community. Whether we meet in a giant cathedral or on the sidewalk, under a brush arbor or in a revival tent, the church is not the facility, but the people who meet in the name of Christ.

Our Lord himself gave the most succinct definition of even the tiniest of churches when he said, "Where two or three are gathered together in my name, there am I in the midst of them."

Jesus said, "Upon this rock I will build my church." The word "church" is the Greek word *ecclesia* and means "called out ones." It has reference to a town meeting or a group of people called to meet for a special purpose. Jesus expressed lordship and partnership with those who were especially called out to meet in his name. Not just any *ecclasia*, but Christ's *ecclasia*, Christ's called out ones.

Beyond the scope of local churches is the marvelous teaching of Christ that all true believers belong to his body, the church, as his espoused bride. This is not, however, to disallow individual believers the responsibility of service in and through local churches.

The bride of Christ is being formed but will not be completed until the last soul is saved before Christ returns to catch his bride away unto himself at the rapture. Until that time, we may best find our avenue of service through identity with a local church. Jesus prayed, "Father, ... I pray ... that they all may be one; ... that the world may believe that thou hast sent me." A New Testament body of believers, functioning in harmony with each other, is both an expression of that unity for which Christ prayed and the ultimate witness of himself to an unbelieving world.

The world does not believe what it cannot see. In the absence of the visible Christ, we who comprise his visible body become a kind of continuing incarnation of Jesus' body on earth. Joined by the purity of the Word and the power of the Spirit to the Head (Christ) in heaven, Jesus lives his life out again through us on earth. A functioning Christian assembly in harmony with itself and her Lord may well be Christ's ultimate witness of himself to lost humanity.

At conversion, Jesus gives each believer a particular kind of spiritual gift to edify his bride, the body. These body-edifying gifts are at once different from and superior to sign gifts which can influence unbelievers. If each member of the body builds up others by the practice of his body-edifying gifts, a healthy body of Christ is established. This body of Christ is far superior as a continuing incarnation of Christ in his witness to the world than any individual sign gift. We may, indeed, do collectively far more than we can accomplish individually.

The apostle Paul spoke clearly to the fruit of the Spirit and the gifts of the Spirit. The various fruits of the Spirit recreate within Christ's body, his own personality of love, joy, and longsuffering. The body-

edifying gifts of the Spirit recreate within the church
the capacity to reproduce the ministry of Christ.
Mercy, giving, encouragement, faith, leadership, and
helps make possible the continuing work of Jesus
through the church.

Perhaps the greatest priority of each believer
should be to join in beseeching the Father to answer
the prayer of our Lord Jesus, "That they all may be
one." Let it be clearly understood that no artificial
union along mere denominational lines is intended. Far
from appealing for denominational union in spite of
doctrinal agreement, we appeal only for unity around
the single issue of doctrinal integrity transcending any
and all denominational structure.

The pitiful human effort to unify Christians in an
end-of-time ecumenical movement is little more than
the foregleams of the Laodicean church age. It is not
for denominational union at any cost that we pray. We
pray for true Christian union about the only stack pole
that is of any value, the purity of the gospel.

While this may be far too much to hope for in our
lifetime, the goal of each church should be to see that
unity around truth within each assembly is achieved.
A divided church is the worst witness a community
can have. Church fights and splits can ruin the testimony of the church for years. Often it is not until a
new generation grows up that never heard about the
old split that a church may redeem her witness in a
community.

The genius of the church, then, must be understood in the mystery of her identity with Christ
through the mystical union of the Holy Spirit. Only as

the Spirit of God is allowed to create that perfect harmony between the Groom and his bride will God's will be done in Christ's earthly body.

Let each of us be committed to the harmony of the church that an unbelieving society may see Christ. This must be the goal of all true believers. It is, indeed, the essence of the mystery of the church.

A Marvelous Truth: The Perpetual Church

Before planets and stars were created, God had the church in mind. Jesus said, "The gates of hell shall not prevail against it." Every passing day gloriously verifies that truth. What the church is, it has been before, and it shall become. No earthly power can stop it, no force of hell can prevail against it. The church is the most powerful, living, vibrant, dynamic force that has ever graced the stage of history.

The mystery then, is not simply our union with Christ and with each other, but with all who have gone before and who will come after. As the pastor of the First Baptist Church of Houston, Texas, I am a member of one particular part of several thousands of Christ's people, comprising a specific segment of his body. But my church is, further, a part of 250 other churches of my denomination in my city, 1,200 in my state and with 35,000 other similar churches in the nation, and 280,000 churches on the North American continent. Beyond this, perhaps a half million churches with hundreds of millions of believers link hands in devotion and commitment to Christ on the earth. Because we exist today, our numbers shall increase tomorrow. Countless millions of yet unborn per-

sons will one day come to know Christ in their generation because we were faithful in ours.

Just so, we owe our very spiritual lives to the
compassion and witness of those who have gone before
us. I am a part of Christ's body now with Peter and
Paul, Savonarola, Martin Luther, John Knox, and
others who have gone before and who served Christ in
the fellowship of his body.

So there is a vertical and horizontal dimension to
the mystery of the church. The church is a union that
transcends boundaries of denomination, time, and history. Believers are mysteriously joined to the living
Christ and to all who are joined, have been joined, and
will be joined to him. The church, then, demands our
highest commitment.

We are inseparably and eternally bound to Christ
and to his church. There is no dividing Christ from his
body—the bride from her groom. I make no apology in
constantly constraining my people to bring the best of
their possessions, time, talents, everything to the
church. Business deals are not as important as the
church. Trips, vacations, plans—nothing—must come
before our commitment to the church.

You cannot love Jesus and not love his bride, the
church. Some people tell me they love Christ but cannot stand the church. That is like saying you love
swimming, but not the water; eating, but not the food;
flying, but not the sky. Impossible!! Paul taught clearly that the mystery of the church is the mystery of its
union as the bride to Christ, her husband. The church
is to be our passion and our priority.

Christ who loved the church and gave himself for

it demands and deserves "a glorious church, not having spot, or wrinkle"—a chaste and pure virgin bride. To love the church is to love the Christ. To love the Christ is to love the church. When you ignore the church, you ignore Jesus. When you criticize the people of God, you criticize their Lord. Christ loved the church. He died for the church. He established the church. He will come back for the church. And to every parachurch group I say loudly and clearly: You will never have the blessing of God without right relationship to his bride, the church. It is one thing to talk about supporting the church; quite another, to give your money, time, and priority to it.

To love the Groom is to love the bride, for her great uniqueness is the mystery of her union with her Lord. If there were a better way to do the will of God and the work of God on earth than through the church of God, the Holy Spirit would have thought of it 2,000 years ago!! Let the parachurch groups take note!

The Mystery of the Church's Foundation

The church's one foundation is Jesus Christ, her Lord. Because he lives, the church lives. Because his truth is marching on, she is unstoppable.

On the surface, a casual reading of Matthew 16:13-18 would appear to indicate that the church is built on Simon Peter.

When Jesus came into the coasts of Caesarea Philippi, he asked his disciples, saying, Whom do men say that I the Son of man am? And they said, Some say that thou art John the Baptist: some, Elias; and others, Jeremias, or one of the prophets. He saith unto them, But whom say ye that I am?

And Simon Peter answered and said, Thou art the Christ, the Son of the living God. And Jesus answered and said unto him, Blessed art thou, Simon Barjona: for flesh and blood hath not revealed it unto thee, but my Father which is in heaven. And I say also unto thee, That thou art Peter, and upon this rock I will build my church; and the gates of hell shall not prevail against it (Matt. 16:13-18).

In truth, however, there is a play on words in the original Greek language. Jesus' statement, "Thou art Peter" is the Greek word *petros*, which means a little rock. Our Lord, then, added, "Upon this rock [Greek *petra*, big rock] I will build my church." Our Lord did not promise to build his church upon Peter, but upon himself. Peter indicated this in his first epistle.

To whom coming, as unto a living stone, disallowed indeed of men, but chosen of God, and precious, Ye also, as lively stones, are built up a spiritual house, an holy priesthood, to offer up spiritual sacrifices, acceptable to God by Jesus Christ. Wherefore also it is contained in the scripture, Behold, I lay in Sion a chief corner stone, elect, precious: and he that believeth on him shall not be confounded. Unto you therefore which believe he is precious: but unto them which be disobedient, the stone which the builders disallowed, the same is made the head of the corner, And a stone of stumbling, and a rock of offence, even to them which stumble at the word, being disobedient: whereunto also they were appointed. But ye are a chosen generation, a royal priesthood, an holy nation, a peculiar people; that ye should shew forth the praises of him who hath called you out of darkness into his marvellous light (1 Pet. 2:4-9).

The Hebrew writer declared that Jesus was a priest forever, after the order of Melchisedec (Heb.

7:17). The uniqueness of Melchisedec's priesthood was that, as far as may be determined from history, he received his priesthood from God and did not pass it on to another person. For eighty generations the Aaronic priesthood received its office by succession and passed it on in the same manner. Our Lord, however, was confirmed the once-for-all high priest for humanity from no one. His eternal priesthood is intrensic within his own being. Nor did he pass it on to another. No one may claim the right of apostolic succession. Christ is our only high priest. He alone is the "one mediator between God and men."

The Mystery of the Church's Preservation

In Ephesians 5:27, God assures his own that he will present to himself "a glorious church, not having spot, or wrinkle, or any such thing."

The final preservation of the saints is assured by an eternal, perpetual Savior. Born in the heart of God, built on the rock, established in living union with Christ, the church will persevere as long as does her Lord! Because he is alive forevermore, we shall live and reign eternally with him. Because he cannot deny himself, his will shall ultimately be accomplished. At the marriage supper of the Lamb, he will present to himself the bride—"a glorious church, not having spot, or wrinkle, or any such thing."

Here is a personal glorious truth: I shall persevere because Christ shall endure. The promise is steadfast. I am complete in him. My final union with him is established forever in the will of God. May I, then, lose my salvation? Only if God ceases to be God, if Jesus is no longer my high priest, if the blood ever loses its power, and if the promises ever lose their faithfulness.

"If in this life only we have hope in Christ, we are of all men most miserable" (1 Cor. 15:19). The best is yet to come for the body of Christ. We look forward to being with Christ forever in heaven. . . . No institution is more beloved of God than the church. No future is more glorious than the church's future. No present is more rewarding and more optimistic than the church's fulfillment of her mission. Given the opportunity to choose between being the President of the United States or some other world-renowned leader, I would rather be a pastor of a church. To paraphrase Edgar A. Guest's "House by the Side of the Road":

Let me have my church on a downtown street
    Where the race of men go by;
The men who are good; the men who are bad
    As good and as bad as I.
I would not sit in the scorner's seat,
    Or hurl the cynics ban,
Let me have my church on Ervay Street
    And be a friend of man.[1]

NOTE

1. W. A. Criswell, *The Doctrine of the Church* (Nashville: Convention Press, 1980), pp. 112-113.

5
The Mystery of
Iniquity

Let no man deceive you by any means: for that day shall not come, except there come a falling away first, and that man of sin be revealed, the son of perdition; Who opposeth and exalteth himself above all that is called God, or that is worshipped; so that he as God sitteth in the temple of God, shewing himself that he is God. Remember ye not, that, when I was yet with you, I told you these things? And now ye know what withholdeth that he might be revealed in his time. For the mystery of iniquity doth already work: only he who now letteth will let, until he be taken out of the way. And then shall that Wicked be revealed, whom the Lord shall consume with the spirit of his mouth, and shall destroy with the brightness of his coming: Even him, whose coming is after the working of Satan with all power and signs and lying wonders, And with all deceivableness of unrighteousness in them that perish; because they received not the love of the truth, that they might be saved. And for this cause God shall send them strong delusion, that they should believe a lie: That they all might be damned who believed not the truth, but had pleasure in unrighteousness (2 Thess. 2:3-12).

Simply stated, 2 Thessalonians 2 deals with the deception of the wicked one perpetrated on the world at the end of the age. Paul looked into the future to say that the Holy Spirit will restrain ("He who now letteth will let") the force of evil until the restraint is taken away at the rapture (v. 8). In the resultant spiritual vacuum at the end of time, Satan will sit down on the throne of David in the form of the Antichrist and declare that he is God (v. 4). At this juncture of world history, the Lord will come and "destroy him with the brightness of His coming" (v. 8).

The events described in 2 Thessalonians 2 were to occur at least nineteen or twenty centuries after Paul wrote them. But Paul's alarming statement is, "The mystery of iniquity doth already work" (v. 7). This amazing fact gives rise to our study in this chapter of the "Mystery of Iniquity." Most of the ability to unlock this mystery lies within these verses.

The Mystery of Iniquity's Perpetuity

Paul looked into the future and said that the final sage of time prior to the return of Christ will be characterized by the permeation of iniquity into every segment of society. But, alas, "The mystery of iniquity doth already work." That which will be, is now (approximately 54 AD), and always has been. Satan's tactics do not change. He who will exalt himself upon David's throne is the eternal pretender to the throne from before the foundation of the world (Isa. 14:12-14). He who would be God tempted Eve to be wise as God and still desires so to be.

If there is one thing you can count on the devil to be, it is the same thing he has always been. Satan's de-

sire to create a world in which man himself becomes
the center of his universe has never changed. Evil is
the same. Evil men are the same, The "mystery of iniquity" which shall work was already at work two thousand years ago and millennia before that.

In many ways, the human race has changed.
Ninety percent of all the scientists who have ever
lived, live today. At this moment in time, the world has
access to more knowledge than was available to all the
preceding generations of history. But our basic problems remain the same. We can put a man on the moon,
but we cannot cure the common cold. We can give a
man the power of presidency, but be shocked as we listen to tapes of his private conversations. We can make
a Ph.D. of an Adolph Eichmann, but be shocked that
he sent six million people to the gas chambers.

No matter how high we go up in scholarship, education, science, astuteness, wealth, and affluence, we
are still the same bunch of liars and thieves we have always been. Our homes are invaded, our women are not
safe on the streets, our children are molested on the
playgrounds, our educators are attacked by those they
would teach. All of this happens in the midst of the
most educated, affluent, powerful, and successful society the world has ever known. The problem? Unregenerate human nature!

"All have sinned, and come short of the glory of
God. We have turned every one to his own way" (Isa.
53:6). We go "astray as soon as [we] be born, speaking
lies" (Ps. 58:3). "Behold I was shapen in iniquity, and
in sin did my mother conceive me" (Ps. 51:5). "There is

none that doeth good, no, not one" (Ps. 14:3). A pseu-
dosophisticated society may scoff at sin and a personal
devil, but our problems are eternal. The sinful nature
of unregenerate humanity is still the cause of the hell
on earth.

Years ago people were given a simple test to de-
termine their sanity. The suspected mentally ill were
placed in a small room with a mop and a bucket. A
stopper was placed in the sink and the faucet turned
on, allowing the water to run over. If the patient
turned off the faucet, he was considered sane. If he
tried to mop up the water, he was too sick to be re-
leased. Society, with its educational process, legisla-
tive directives, and social programs has, for centuries,
been attempting to mop up the water of social disor-
der, crime, and sin. Those who would turn off the
water are branded "religious fanatics." Sinful nature,
apart from the saving grace of Jesus Christ, does not
change. The "mystery of iniquity" is, in part, the mystery of its perpetuity.

The Mystery of Iniquity's Deception

In verses 2-3, Paul eluded to a probable fake letter
or message sent to the church at Thessalonica. Paul
was apparently attempting to diffuse the teaching of
an impostor, who was declaring that the "day of Christ
is at hand." Someone pretending to represent Paul's
apostolic authority was leading the church to believe
the coming of Christ had already occurred and they
had missed it.

This was, of course, a blatant and flagrant lie. But
we ought not be surprised at this, for it is the nature of

iniquity to be deceptive. The very word *Lucifer* means light-bearer or one who shines. Sin is never as it appears to be. Evil's representation is often in the guise of the person of distinction. But the person of distinction today is often "the person of extinction" tomorrow.

In verse 11, Paul referred to Satan as "the lie." The King James Version says "a lie," but the original manuscripts contain the definite article "the lie." "The lie" perpetrates power, signs, and lying wonders (v. 9) of the deceivableness of unrighteousness (v. 10) allowed by God (v. 11) because they refuse to receive the truth (v. 10). The result? "That they all might be damned who believed not the truth, but had pleasure in unrighteousness" (v. 12). Which will you believe, "the Truth" which is Christ, or "the lie," the devil? Whom will you serve? The decision is yours. But Satan is a liar, and his strength is in his deception. You cannot win at the game of sin. You cannot break the laws of God. You can only break yourself upon them, maybe not today or tomorrow, but eventually sin will destroy you.

Few things have deceived as many as alcohol. "Ah," but many say, "only one out of sixteen who drink become alcoholics." Suppose you were to go to the airport and buy a ticket to fly to New York City. Before issuing the ticket the agent said, "We are obligated to tell you that one out of sixteen seats on the plane will fall out sometime during the flight." Would you board the flight? Probably not because the odds are too great. But the odds against winning at sin are even greater. Don't be deceived by the evil one. The odds of beating iniquity's deception are a billion to zero. What chance has the sinner to win at sin? He has no chance at all.

The Mystery of Iniquity's Openness

While Satan is the master of deception, the blatancy and openness of his approach will increase toward the end of time. Our Lord taught that "because iniquity shall abound, the love of many shall wax cold" (Matt. 4:12). Evil, at the end of time, will abound and get out of bounds. The abounding, unbridled presence of evil is everywhere. Would you have believed ten years ago that today you would sit in your living room and allow the words to come into your home that come through your television set? Students have begun doing in junior high what they only used to do in college and in grade school, what used to go on only in high school. A New York City agency is training teachers to detect the presence of drug usage in preschoolers.

Sin is out of bounds. It is not simply in the brothel, skid row, and the bars. It is in the schools, in the homes, in the churches — it is everywhere. Sit down for an hour and listen carefully to every word of the rock-and-roll songs your teenagers hear all day long. You will be shocked.

On November 6, 1979, the city of San Francisco voted on a city ordinance to do away with the vice squad. Police were to have nothing to do with enforcing laws against homosexuality, prostitution, gambling, and pornography. One journalist said that if the ordinance were passed, San Francisco would become "THE WHOREHOUSE OF THE NATION." Fortunately, the ordinance was soundly defeated, but it is a sign of the times. This is the character of an anything-goes society that shall mark that generation which exists right before the coming of Christ.

The Independence of Iniquity

Characteristically evil acts on its own. "We will not have this man to reign over us" was the cry of the Jews. But they spoke for us all, for it is intrinsic to the nature of iniquity that it rebels against the authority of God and will act in independence. Characteristic of the final age of time will be a permeating presence in society to "do its own thing." It's an old problem. For in the wilderness, every man "did that which was right in his own eyes."

In verse 3, the Thessalonians were warned that the "day of Christ" will be preceded by a "falling away." That is a perfect description of sin. Sin is to pull away from God, and "falling away" indicates a downward fall. The only way people may go when they choose to go away from God is down. Jonah went down to Tarshish; Samson went down to Timnath; David looked down from the rooftop and lusted after beautiful Bath-sheba.

Intrinsic to the nature of sin is the tendency to rebellion. Independent action from God is always there. The hiss of the serpent may always be heard, "Eat thereof, then your eyes shall be opened, and ye shall be as gods."

The Influence of Iniquity

If the influence of good is strong (and it is), it would appear that the influence of evil is greater. The good apples must work much more diligently to offset the harm done by the one rotten apple which spoils the barrel. The influence of evil has far-reaching effects. How far-reaching are evil's tenacles? It is to "them that perish" and "they who receive not the love of the truth, that they might be saved" (v. 10). "For this cause God shall send them strong delusion, that they should believe a lie" (v. 11), and that "they all might be damned" (v. 12).

Our Lord warned in the Second Commandment that, if his followers falsely represent him, certain forces would be set in operation to affect descendants "unto the third and fourth generation" (Ex. 20:5).

The biblical warning is, "Be sure your sin will find you out." Notice that it does not say, "Your sin will be found out." Rather, "Your sin will find you out." There is a vast difference. Your sin may never be found out. No one may ever know, but it will become a part of your personality, your body, your eyes, your spirit, and be reflected in your children. The lingering effects of the influence of evil are awesome things and greatly to be feared.

The Mystery of Iniquity's Attraction

The bottom line of the issue is that the strong majority have had "pleasure in unrighteousness," rejected the truth, and are eternally damned (v. 12). How can such a thing be? To my own heart, the greatest mystery of iniquity is the mystery of its attractiveness. We know Satan's deception; we know his craftiness; we know the finished product of his crafty art. We know the wages of sin is death. We know, as well, the awesome price paid by our Lord to deliver us from evil. The great mystery, then, is this: Why do we sin at all?

Before us are set two choices: the way of life and death; the way of iniquity and the way of godliness. Heaven and hell are before us, eternal perdition or blessing. The wonder of wonders is that man would choose evil knowing what he knows, willingly sacrificing all to "enjoy the pleasures of sin for a season." Contemplate your ways. Let the Spirit of God and the Word of God, let alone your own experience and common sense, expose the evil one for what he is — a fraud.

Rhea F. Miller has described so beautifully the options that are the believer's. May his choice be ours.

> I'd Rather Have Jesus than silver or gold,
> I'd rather be His than have riches untold,
> I'd Rather Have Jesus than houses or lands,
> I'd rather be led by His nail-pierced hand
>
> I'd Rather Have Jesus than men's applause,
> I'd rather be faithful to His dear cause,
> I'd Rather Have Jesus than worldwide fame,
> I'd rather be true to His holy name
>
> Than to be the king of a vast domain,
> Or be held in sin's dread sway.
> I'd Rather Have Jesus than anything
> This world affords today.[1]

NOTE

1. "I'd Rather Have Jesus" © Copyright 1922 by Rhea Florence Miller. Copyright Renewal 1950 by Rhea Florence Miller. Copyright 1939 by George Beverly Shea. Words by Rhea Florence Miller. Music by George Beverly Shea. Used by permission of Chancel Music, Inc., Western Springs, Illinois.

6
The Mystery of
Godliness

These things write I unto thee, hoping to come unto thee shortly: But if I tarry long, that thou mayest know how thou oughtest to behave thyself in the house of God, which is the church of the living God, the pillar and ground of the truth. And without controversy great is the mystery of godliness: God was manifest in the flesh, justified in the Spirit, seen of angels, preached unto the Gentiles, believed on in the world, received up into glory (1 Tim. 3:14-16).

The Scriptures constantly set before us the extremes that a person may choose. There is the possibility of heaven and hell, the privilege of choosing life or death. We may follow the crooked way or the straight; the narrow road, or the broad way. The way to life is as far removed from the way to death as is the East from the West. But there is always a point at which the two are very close. At the earliest moral junctions of our lives, we may stand in one spot and choose to live out the crooked way or the straight. Eternity with or without God, while set milleniums apart, was once within easy grasp of all. We do well to teach our children that *the broad way gets narrower* and *the narrow way gets wider.*

Perhaps no greater contrast, however, can be made than the one between the mystery of iniquity and the mystery of godliness. In his first letter to Timothy, Paul was writing to a young preacher boy who was his own understudy and, quite possibly, the pastor of a church. Paul attempted, among other things, to explain how Timothy, as a spiritual leader, should behave among the family of God. At the conclusion of chapter 3 Paul made it clear that there was no question to the truth that the summation of it all is the godliness seen in Timothy's life.

As the perfect antithesis to the mystery of iniquity, godliness may well be, to an iniquitous world, the deepest mystery of all the behavior of the family of God. Nowhere more than in Paul's letters to Timothy may the mystery of godliness fully be seen. Let us examine what Paul had to say about godliness to the young preacher.

Godliness Is Related to Quietness

In 1 Timothy 6:6 Paul's comment, "godliness with contentment is great gain" simply told Timothy that godliness and contentment go together. To the world possession is contentment; money and prestige are contentment; success and sin are contentment. But Paul said that contentment is related to godliness.

In 1 Timothy 2:2 Paul said that a quiet and peaceful life go with godliness and honesty. Goodness and happiness are inseparably bound together. The person with a beautiful, quiet spirit that runs deep is often the godliest of all. Jesus Christ was the most hassled, har-

ried, tested, and tried man that ever lived. But in the
midst of it all, he had the composure and sweetness of
life in perfect harmony with the Father.

In the second chapter of his first letter to Timothy, Paul urged Timothy to exhort the women
members (v. 9-10) to make their godliness known with
the internal beauty of a quiet spirit. The beauty of the
Christian woman is the loveliness of her quiet spirit.
No greater attractiveness may be found than the
charm of such a woman in harmony with God and in
tune with her world. Paul was not denouncing make-
up, fixing hair, or wearing jewelry. Rather, he was
saying that these things ought not to be considered
the most beautiful things in their lives. This prestig-
ious quality is reserved for the inner beauty of the
spirit. A woman's queenly and regal-like manner is but
the manifestation of a godly nature intrinsic within
her very being.

But if women are more inclined to relate beauty to
contentment, men are presupposed to identify mate-
rial gain with contentment. But Paul said that physical wealth does not bring contentment; these two do
not stand hand in hand. But just as beauty and godliness are bound together, so are fulfillment and righteousness. To find real beauty, then, is to find the Master. To know true success is to know the Lord. Beauty,
peace, and fulfillment stand hand in hand with righteousness. Godliness is related to quiet contentment.

Godliness Is Related to Truth

This know also, that in the last days perilous times shall
come. For men shall be lovers of their own selves, covetous,

boasters, proud, blasphemers, disobedient to parents, un-
thankful, unholy, Without natural affection, trucebreakers,
false accusers, incontinent, fierce, despisers of those that are
good. Traitors, heady, highminded, lovers of pleasures more
than lovers of God; Having a form of godliness, but denying
the power thereof: from such turn away. For of this sort are
they which creep into houses, and lead captive silly women
laden with sins, led away with divers lusts, Ever learning,
and never able to come to the knowledge of the truth (2 Tim.
3:1-7).

Paul's word translated "silly" does not mean
giddy or foolish, as we think of it today. The word
means "without information." "Ignorant" is a more
accurate translation. The problem with the world is
that it is uninformed about truth. There is no new
birth—only outward religion. There is only a form of
godliness in the world without the new birth and
power of the Spirit. There are amens and benedictions,
but little heart conversion. Nothing falls into place in a
decadent, off-centered society because absolutes have
evaporated in a vacuum of ignorance.

Without truth there can be no righteousness.
Every person becomes a law unto himself without the
truth of God's law, and the result is social anarchy and
moral chaos. Society cannot live out the basis of moral
truth and expect to build anything except the kind of
world described in 2 Timothy 2.

If the foundation is lacking, the whole house will
be crooked. Paul described the complete social havoc
that will characterize humanity at the end of world history. Why? Because this is the kind of society that
leads people by their moral noses into sin and divers

lust because it cannot and will not learn the truth. We are spinning our collective wheels in attempting to solve the problems of a sick society without rebuilding her moral foundations in the truth of the Word of God. Much of the mystery of godliness may be seen in the fact that the godly know and do the truth, while the ungodly refuse to hear it.

Godliness Is Related to Separation

One of the most stirring challenges to godliness in the New Testament is Paul's exhortation to young Timothy to have the Christian fortitude to separate himself from the world and unto Christ.

Thou therefore, my son, be strong in the grace that is in Christ Jesus. And the things that thou hast heard of me among many witnesses, the same commit thou to faithful men, who shall be able to teach others also. Thou therefore endure hardness, as a good soldier of Jesus Christ. No man that warreth entangleth himself with the affairs of this life; that he may please him who hath chosen him to be a soldier (2 Tim. 2:1-4).

Godliness is, in part, simply bearing a quality that is Godlike. It has strong overtones of distinctiveness, difference, and separation about it. The godly will not live like the ungodly. The sinner does not live like the righteous. The spiritual person may not be found in worldly places frequented by the carnal person. One of the purposes of the civil law, with its microscopic attention to detail, was to create an atmosphere in which Israel was constantly making choices. They had to forever breathe in a moral climate that recognized a difference in what may and may not be done. It was true

in law, in diet, in worship, in relationships, in everything. Society says anything goes. God says some
things are forbidden. Not everything is all right for
everybody.

Universalism has long since abandoned the moral
pegs of the Judeo-Christian faith. But what you believe does make a difference. We are not free to choose
our own life-styles and do our own things. If we would
please God, we must obey him. Godliness is absolutely
related to holiness, and holiness means separation. We
don't like to hear much about dancing, smoking, cus-
sing, drinking, gambling, dirty movies, poker, and so
forth. That's old-fashioned and fundamentalist. But it
is true, nonetheless, that God expects his people to be
different from the worldly people. Godliness is related
to separation.

O ye sons of men, how long will ye turn my glory into
shame? how long will ye love vanity, and seek after leasing?
Selah. But know that the Lord hath set apart him that is
godly for himself: the Lord will hear when I call unto him.
Stand in awe, and sin not: commune with your own heart
upon your bed, and be still. Selah. Offer the sacrifices of
righteousness, and put your trust in the Lord (Ps. 4:2-5).

Not only is there a difference in the way the godly
treat the world but also there is a marked difference in
the way the world treats the godly. Listen again to
Paul's strong pronouncement in 2 Timothy 3:12-15:

Yea, and all that will live godly in Christ Jesus shall suffer
persecution. But evil men and seducers shall wax worse and
worse, deceiving, and being deceived. But continue thou in
the things which thou hast learned and hast been assured of,

knowing of whom thou hast learned them; And that from a child thou hast known the holy scriptures, which are able to make thee wise unto salvation through faith which is in Christ Jesus (2 Tim. 3:12-15).

The price to be paid for following Christ is separation from the world. Obedience to those things we have learned from childhood will cost us something. "All [not just a few] that will live godly in Christ Jesus shall suffer persecution." The righteous person makes the world feel guilty. The Christian makes the world uneasy. Why are worldly people miserable? Because they are a whole lot guilty and a little bit envious. But by our godly lives and accompanying testimony, we shall win them over.

But, as we have seen in the mystery of Christ's body, the church, an unbelieving world will never be attracted to a Christ represented by people who live as the world lives. There is enough of the folly of divisiveness and futility of sin in the world to disillusion sinners and send them scurrying after something else.

But to whom shall they go? Where shall they look? Will it not be toward us only if we are different than they? The world already knows that what it has does not satisfy. If it is to seek satisfaction in what we have found, it must see a difference. Much of the mystery of godliness is in the godlikeness of separation to be seen in the life of the believer.

Godliness Is Related to Jesus Christ

The clear teaching of the Scriptures is that humans, having no righteousness of their own, can only stand in right relationship to God on the basis of an imputed righteousness through faith in Christ. Our godliness, then, is intrinsically bound up in the character of Jesus. If he were not fully and completely God himself, there is no efficacy in him to impute a godly character to us.

Paul's commentary on the mystery of godliness, as recorded in 1 Timothy 3:16, must be viewed not as a definition of godliness, but as the basis for the imputation of godliness to ungodly men. People receive this godliness through believing in the incarnation, death, and resurrection of him who was deity personified: God manifest in the flesh. "And without controversy great is the mystery of godliness: God was manifest in the flesh, justified in the Spirit, seen of angels, preached unto the Gentiles, believed on in the world, received up into glory" (1 Tim. 3:16).

The capacity of Christ to impute his godliness to me is contingent upon his deity. What he purposes to do for me may be validated exclusively upon the basis of what God has done in him. The incarnation of God—attested to by the Holy Spirit, seen before creation in the presence of angels—is the testimony of the Scriptures. But, further, the power of Jesus' death and resurrection, the basis of salvation, has been declared to the world, validated by the transformation of response, and acknowledged in heaven at the ascension where Jesus' blood was sprinkled on the mercy seat and the Son forever seated at the right hand of the Father.

In short, from the foundation of the world until the salvation of the last person who will ever believe, the mystery of the godliness of man stands exclusively in relationship to the mystery of the imputed godliness of Jesus who is at once eternal Author and Creator, incarnate Sacrifice and Justifier of all.

What is the mystery of godliness? It is simply stated that God, in Christ, will impute to every man on the basis of faith, the divine nature of him who is God incarnate in a man. My commitment to Christ must be total, complete, and separate from the world, emanating in a beautiful and quiet spirit that is rooted in the truth of his Word.

7
The Mystery of
the Faith

This is a true saying, If a man desire the office of a bishop, he desireth a good work. A bishop then must be blameless, the husband of one wife, vigilant, sober, of good behaviour, given to hospitality, apt to teach; Not given to wine, no striker, not greedy of filthy lucre; but patient, not a brawler, not covetous; One that ruleth well his own house, having his children in subjection with all gravity; (For if a man know not how to rule his own house, how shall he take care of the church of God?) Not a novice, lest being lifted up with pride he fall into the condemnation of the devil. Moreover he must have a good report of them which are without; lest he fall into reproach and the snare of the devil. Likewise must the deacons be grave, not double-tongued, not given to much wine, not greedy of filthy lucre; Holding the mystery of the faith in a pure conscience. And let these also first be proved; then let them use the office of a deacon, being found blameless. Even so must their wives be grave, not slanderers, sober, faithful in all things. Let the deacons be the husbands of one wife, ruling their children and their own houses well. For they that have used the office of a deacon well purchase to themselves a good degree, and great boldness in the faith which is in Christ Jesus (1 Tim. 3:1-13).

Paul's first letter to Timothy deals, at great length, with the qualifications of spiritual leadership. Perhaps that which comes through the strongest is the emphasis upon spiritual maturity. Graveness, sobriety, not a novice, the appropriate spiritual maturity of his own family are all characteristics which may only come with age. Surely the apostle had this in mind when he advised the church to "lay hands suddenly on no man" (1 Tim. 5:22).

Undoubtedly the most controversial qualification has been, "the husband of one wife" (v. 2). While Paul may have been referring to divorce and remarriage, I think this is not necessarily the case. It would appear that while we do require much of our spiritual leaders, it is unfortunate that we assume the gospel of the second chance seems incapable of handling the problem of divorce and remarriage. This is particularly true in the case of a deacon who was divorced because his wife broke the sexual commitment of the marriage vow.

At any rate, most commentators (and I concur) feel that the reference to "one wife" is a reference to bigamy. In most of the mission fields of the world, even to this day, bigamy is a very real problem. The predominance of bigamy in most of the countries of the world place the church in a difficult situation. Even those cultures who practice it lose respect for the church if they receive into their membership a new Christian man married to two women. If he is to separate himself from one of his wives, the question then becomes which. And to even begin to attempt to resolve the matter usually means forcing the divorced wife into prostitution to survive financially. Paul, then, may have been addressing himself to a very real problem.

The purpose of this chapter is to address ourselves to the issue of the mystery of the faith. This is, perhaps, the least emphasized of all the qualifications. But it may be the most important for one who would serve as a deacon. Notice that the qualification "holding the mystery of the faith in a pure conscience" (v. 9) is added just for the deacon and is not specifically stated for the bishop. The term "bishop" may be used interchangeably with *elder, overseer,* and possibly even *pastor.* It appears, then, that Paul assumed that a minister has a good grasp of the mystery of the faith. The specific direction of this Scripture passage is that we be exceedingly certain to discern that those to be ordained as deacons have a full grasp of "the mystery of the faith." It may well be that the apparent emphasis upon maturity makes impossible the achieving of this quality in youth. While occasionally young men may be found to have an unusual spiritual maturity, for the most part, it comes with age.

Some of the earlier manuscripts do not contain the definite article *the* but simply state "holding the mystery of faith." The expression "the faith," however, appears to be more in keeping with the general qualifications being outlined in context in the letter to Timothy. The simple teaching of this Scripture passage is that spiritual leadership must have a good grasp of the mystery of the faith and that in a good conscience.

What, then, may we assume the faith to be? Apparently this beautiful expression refers to everything

that is related to the Christian religion. That is not to
say that a deacon must be versed in Greek and Hebrew to serve. It does mean that a deacon will have a
kind of grasp of apologetics, church history, and sound
doctrine. We are not saying that seminary courses are
required or that specific dates and theologies must be
memorized. We are saying that a person must be able
to defend the faith, know the superiority of Christianity to any other philosophy, and have a profound understanding of where we are as the people of God and
what we are doing as his children.

We often say, "keep the faith" or "be true to the
faith." In so doing, we speak of a whole grasp of the
spiritual concepts that are unique to Christ and his
church. The scholarly-oriented person is not necessarily prepared to be a deacon. One who would attempt to operate the church of God on the same principles as a business is ill-prepared for spiritual leadership. There is a charm and uniqueness, an eternal
mystique, a spiritual dimension about "the faith" that
is different from anything and everything else. The
church budget is not operated in the same manner
that General Motors operates its budget. There is a
kind of heavenly table of mathematics about the
things of God that General Motors does not understand. We receive by giving, we live by dying, we do
not give God one day a week and have six left over. In
zest, life, service, and time, we are left with eight or
ten or twelve in giving the one to Him. Ten dollars
minus one dollar leaves nine dollars in a secular society. But in the things of God, it leaves twelve dollars or
fifteen dollars.

The pastor of the church is the leader, yet the servant of all. The deacons often operate the business of the church but are, in fact, the servants of the church. The body itself is the ultimate authority in the decision-making process, but it is they who are led by an undershepherd. It sounds like a merry-go-round, doesn't it? This is a concept the world cannot understand, one by which the world cannot operate. For in the world, superiority is of prime importance; pride would make such an operation impossible. But in the body of Christ our charter is different: "In honour preferring one another." There is no way to explain how all of this works; but where the Spirit of Christ is in control, it does work.

At this very moment, our church is on the verge of a dream of several years in the making—being able to give a million dollars a year to missions. In so doing, the phenomenon has occurred that the church's own personal income has increased 2,000 percent in the last decade. The more we give, the more we have. Impossible? Yes, to a Ph.D. in mathematics, but not to an humble congregation of believers in Christ.

This is part of the mystery of the faith, it is that different dimension that prepares a man for spiritual leadership. "The faith" is all that we are and do and believe as the body of Christ. It is the spirit, the dynamism, the priority, the mission, the purpose, the fellowship, the essence of our very existence, and a deacon must grasp it well.

Undoubtedly, it is an understanding to which a person may not come in the infancy of his spiritual pilgrimage. The novice must not be placed in leadership.

The new convert must not be cast suddenly into the vulnerable position of giving direction in things he has not had time to understand. The new wine must not be placed in old skins.

Everything about the Christian faith is different. We do not need the secular, the immature, or the worldly making our decisions for us. "Brother goeth to law with brother, and that before the unbelievers" (1 Cor. 6:6).

As I thought about the mystery of the faith, I could not help but think of the faces of five or ten of my finer, older deacons who have demonstrated their deep insight into "the mystery of the faith." They are the kinds of men every pastor needs and upon whom he regularly depends for counsel and advice. In thinking about the qualifications, the personality, ministry, and service of these good men, three characteristics common to all express evidence that they hold "the mystery of the faith."

An Enduring Quality

The mature Christian takes the long look. He does not panic when things are going badly, nor is he overjoyed when there appears to be an excess abundance of provision. His attitude is that God is in control, and things will even out. The Book which is the basis of our faith is not, after all, the book of the month; it is "the Book of the ages." The church of the Lord Jesus will survive. He will not forsake his own. He who said, "Upon this rock I will build my church, and the gates of hell shall not prevail against it," is still the living Lord of his people. What we do and are must always be understood in terms of what we have been since the

New Testament era and what we shall be until the coming of Christ.

The mature person never makes childish judgments. The chief characteristic of childhood is to take the short look. The child wants that which pleases right now. As a child, I used to await eagerly the continuation of serials at the local moviehouse from Saturday afternoon to Saturday afternoon. The hero was always left in a perplexing situation with the only promise "To Be Continued Next Week." "Next week" always brought victory and deliverance.

The mature believer, in spite of present conditions, has turned to the last chapter of the Book and knows that everything will come out all right. The game is not over at halftime. The believer walks *through* "the valley of the shadow of death." He does not stay in it.

One of my more mature deacons happens to be a young man. When we relocated our church, we had great difficulty in selling our old property. Often in my anxiety I would ask him to "do something to hasten the sale." Deliberations were long and difficult, and I wanted it done yesterday. Repeatedly, he would assure me by saying, "Pastor, I feel we are right where we should be at this particular time in the negotiations." The person with a good grasp of the faith takes a comprehensive look at the whole, knows that God is in control, does not panic, and is content to say: "We are perfectly in the center of his will. We are exactly what and where we should be at this particular time."

For many years, I have enjoyed the fellowship of my dear friend, Charles Allen of our sister congregation, the First Methodist Church of Houston. A few years ago a young spiritual leader named "Guru Maharajah Ji" came to Houston with thousands of his followers for a giant meeting in the Astrodome. I was very concerned that perhaps we should offset his appearance with advertising, demonstrators, and so forth. Allen's wise counsel was, "John, the churches of Houston have been preaching the gospel of Christ for nearly a century and a half. We have been here before he came, and will be here long after he is gone." Allen was right. The young guru's ministry was no more than a passing fancy and is today a dead issue in Houston and in the world.

Those who hold the mystery of the faith in a pure conscience have an enduring quality in their perception of the things of God. Faith takes the long look, faith does not panic, faith lets God be God.

My father-in-law, approaching eighty years of age, has been preaching the gospel for sixty years. While I was still in college, he made what appeared to me to be a very rash statement. "John," he said, "you are a young man with a long way to go and much promise for the Lord's work. But be true and take your time. Remember this: Only one out of ten who start out in the work of God at age twenty-one will end up in it at age sixty-five." Mentally I challenged that statement. In the back of an old Bible, I wrote down the names of twenty-four young men my age who were becoming prominent in Christian work. At this writing, only twenty-five years have transpired, and I am forty-five. I am sad to say that, as of today, only three of those twenty-four names are still in full-time Christian work.

An Eternal Quality

Everything the mature person of God does has about it the touch of the eternal, the touch of the spiritual over the temporal. All things physical are viewed as only vehicles for spiritual good. A business, to the spiritually mature person, is not a tool for selfish gain. It is an instrument to do the will of God. A house is not a showcase to impress business associates; it is a home where children may be nurtured in the things of God. A business luncheon is not primarily a place to make a deal, but an opportunity to share Christ. Ironically, in the process, the deal will normally be made and a better deal than the Christian could have made on his own. The reason? "Seek ye first the kingdom of God, and his righteousness; and all these things shall be added unto you" (Matt. 6:33).

I am thinking specifically of Cy Perkins, a deacon in our church. He is the kind of man who, if you ask to pray for you, will stop and say, "I certainly will. Let's pray right now." He never fails to approach any life situation without spiritual discernment. "What is God doing here? What would he have me do? What may I do for him?" This is a kind of spiritual maturation which, unfortunately, few achieve. But, oh, what blessings are these kinds of people to their pastors, their churches, and to their Lord.

An Endearing Quality

By "an endearing quality," I refer to the genuine love held uniquely by the mature believer for the things of God.

Recently a man employed full time by one of the

parachurch groups discussed with me how much he loved our church and how equal was his commitment to it and to his own ministry. I thought of the words of our Lord, "Where your treasure is, there will your heart be also," and examined his giving record. In the past year and a half he had given $126. My point? Simply this: There comes a time in the life of the mature believer where he doesn't just sing "Take my silver and my gold," but he actually means it from his heart and lives that way.

One of the great verses of the Scriptures is Luke 6:38: "Give, and it shall be given unto you; good measure, pressed down, and shaken together, and running over, shall men give into your bosom. For with the same measure that ye mete withal it shall be measured to you again." It is wonderful to hear a congregation say amen when the pastor quotes that verse. It is quite another thing when a people of God actually live by it. It is one thing to sing, "If Jesus Goes with Me, I'll Go Anywhere" and "Wherever He Leads I'll Go." It is quite another thing to actually go.

The mature believer may best be characterized by his love for the Lord. But it is not a soupy, sentimental kind of love that makes your hair stand up on the back of your neck when you sing, "Onward, Christian Soldiers" that makes the difference. It is the kind of love that does what it says it believes. Love is something you do.

One of the finest Christian laymen I have ever known is a very wealthy man. I do not know how much he owns, and I do not think he knows. Just one of his businesses has 150 businesses within it. I know that he sits on at least sixty boards of directors and trustees, but I have never seen him miss Bible study on Wednesday night or a deacon's meeting or a church service. Many times he has flown out of the way on a trip from Denver or Seattle to Washington, DC, just to be in his own church on Wednesday night in Houston. He is a man to whom the things of God are very dear. There is an endearing quality about spiritual maturity.

Some years ago an Oklahoma Indian was asked to move to Arizona to work for an oil company. The man was a Christian and taught a men's Sunday School class in a small Baptist church in the Sooner State for years. His rapport with Indian people and knowledge of many Indian dialects would make him an invaluable asset in dealing with the Indians of Arizona. When he declined even to consider the position, the financial offer was increased repeatedly. Finally they handed him a blank check and said, "Name your figure." Even then the answer was still no. "That's not the problem," he said. "The first offer you made was much more than I make now. My Sunday School class is the most important thing in the world to me. Your salary is big enough, but your job isn't."

That Christian Indian Sunday School teacher had an endearing quality about his life relative to the things of God. Out of that class, not incidentally, through the years, came more than forty men who became preachers and missionaries. "Your salary is big enough, but your job isn't." What a profound statement. What a dynamic illustration of the truth of the endearing quality about the things of God to the spiritually mature believer who holds "the mystery of the faith in a good conscience."

8
The Mystery of
Transformation

And we know that all things work together for good to them that love God, to them who are the called according to his purpose. For whom he did foreknow, he also did predestinate to be conformed to the image of his Son, that he might be the firstborn among many brethren. Moreover whom he did predestinate, them he also called: and whom he called, them he also justified: and whom he justified, them he also glorified. What shall we then say to these things? If God be for us, who can be against us? . . . Who shall separate us from the love of Christ? Shall tribulation, or distress, or persecution, or famine, or nakedness, or peril, or sword? As it is written, For thy sake we are killed all the day long; we are accounted as sheep for the slaughter. Nay, in all these things we are more than conquerors through him that loved us. For I am persuaded, that neither death, nor life, nor angels, nor principalities, nor powers, nor things present, nor things to come, nor height, nor depth, nor any other creature, shall be able to separate us from the love of God, which is in Christ Jesus our Lord (Rom. 8:28-31,35-37).

Of all the mysteries in the Bible, one of the most intriguing and most complicated is the mystery of transformation. The mystery of transformation is that fantastic work of God that begins at the moment of salvation and continues until we become like unto our Lord in every aspect of our lives. Paul wrote, "Being confident of this very thing, that he which hath begun a good work in you will perform it until the day of Jesus Christ" (Phil. 1:6). The word "perform" used here is that word which speaks of maturity. God begins his work of salvation and maturing us one minute at a time, one day at a time through the power of the indwelling Spirit of Christ. In Philippians 2, we read, "For it is God which worketh in you both to will and to do of his good pleasure."

Part of the mystery of transformation is that God would even choose to place his workshop within a weakened, troubled tabernacle such as sinful humanity. The mystery of transformation is couched with the unfathomable depths of God's love and grace. We are saved by God's grace. God loves us and gave himself for us. But God's love is so rich and full that he longs to finish the work within us which he has begun.

Man's love is so often nearsighted, short-term, and inconclusive. It is often filled with the now and today, but cares not for the later, tomorrow, and the forever. Man's love is primarily self-centered. God's love, *agape* love, is self-emptying. The mystery of transformation says that this God who loves will not withhold any good thing from them that walk uprightly.

God has assured us repeatedly that no one who comes to him will be cast out. "My sheep know my voice, and I know them." Within the fantastic, limitless boundaries of his love, his work of grace is perfected in us and through us by the mystery of transformation.

The story was told of two caterpillars crawling across the ground. They both looked overhead and saw a butterfly. One caterpillar nudged the other and said, "You couldn't get me up in one of those things for a million dollars!" The point is obvious. The God who knew, planned, and prepared for me, even before my formation in the womb, knowing what was best for me, has begun a work of grace that will eventually transform me into the image of his dear Son.

I read not long ago an article in the *Houston Post* which carried the headline, "Nightmare Over Skylab Kills Man in Philippines." A fifty-eight-year-old Filipino man died of a heart attack shouting, "Skylab! Skylab!" in his sleep. The front-page story said Simeon G. Galvez was stricken in Valenauela, north of Manila, as a result of the nightmare. How futile and destructive are our fears!

Yet so often we mortals fear and tremble, day in and day out, not knowing that all that God is doing is for our good, part of his tremendous plan of transformation. The promise rings loud and clear. "Fear thou not; for I am with thee. Be not dismayed; for I am thy God. I will strengthen thee; yea, I will help thee; yea, I will uphold thee with the right hand of my righteousness."

Another part of the mystery of transformation deals with the fact that in the midst of our changing, God is changeless. The writer of Hebrews spoke of Christ as the same yesterday, today, and forever. We are reminded repeatedly that he is our ultimate aim, the Source and Sustenance of life itself.

As we move progressively toward God, we see the clarity of his consistency. We march from sinful immaturity to sinless maturity.

For the grace of God that bringeth salvation hath appeared to all men, Teaching us that, denying ungodliness and worldly lusts, we should live soberly, righteously, and godly, in this present world; Looking for that blessed hope, and the glorious appearing of the great God and our Saviour Jesus Christ; Who gave himself for us, that he might redeem us from all iniquity, and purify unto himself a peculiar people, zealous of good works. These things speak, and exhort, and rebuke with all authority. Let no man despise thee (Titus 2:11-15).

The Christian marches to the beat of the drum of the Spirit of God implanted in the soul of every believer. The rate of spiritual maturity is often related to the degree of sensitivity to the Spirit of God embodied within the believer. The drums of deception and deceit dramatically dare us to depart from the direction of discipleship. The devil is the great deceiver, the author and father of lies, the counterfeit of all creation.

Transformation, then, is to become like Jesus. To be like Jesus means that we must know him. We must know his Word, which means we must spend time in his Word. Jesus said, "I am the way, the truth, and the life." As the disciples learned of him, their lives were changed. In the last chapter of the Gospel of John, Jesus thrice questioned Peter in relationship to his devotion, saying, "Lovest thou me?" Peter's response, "Yea, Lord; thou knowest that I love thee," came after many days of learning who Jesus really was. That ex-

periential love came from personal experiences with
the Master. Peter knew Christ and loved him, and
Peter's life had been changed. The wild-eyed, coarse-
handed fisherman was now a different man. The mystery of transformation was in progress. God was at
work.

To be like Jesus is to be transformed. To be transformed, we must know him. To know Jesus is to love
him. Paul, as a veteran of the cross, was longing late in
life for God to complete the perfect work of grace
which he had begun. Paul had not arrived. He was still
en route to the full accomplishment of God's transformation. Paul said, "Brethren, I count not myself to
have apprehended; but this one thing I do, forgetting
those things which are behind, and reaching forth
unto those things which are before, I press toward the
mark for the prize of the high calling of God in Christ
Jesus" (Phil. 3:13-14).

The mystery of transformation involves the
matchless grace and bountiful love of Jesus Christ and
man's willingness to be conformed or be transformed
into the image of Christ. True transformation involves
a personal awareness of the fact that "if any man be in
Christ, he is a new creature: old things are passed
away; behold, all things are become new" (2 Cor. 5:17).
The mystery of transformation is to be like Jesus in
relationship to his desires, his presence, and his transformed, glorified body.

The pinnacle of transformation will mean that we
will have a body that cannot sin, a body that cannot
suffer, a body that cannot sorrow, and a body that is
not susceptible to the weak and beggary ailments of a

sin-soaked society. Jesus came out of the grave with a glorified body, perfect and whole. The Bible says we shall be like him. Someday all perfection of God's creation will bring forth a personal, glorified body for every believer.

I marvel every time I look at pictures of our new facilities completed in April of 1977, when we relocated six miles west of our downtown location. Many pictures that were taken show the rough, stark, steel beams with no doors or windows. I stand amazed at how such a shabby, shattered piece of nothingness can become a beautiful edifice to the glory of God. As a believer in Christ, I am inseparably linked to ultimate reality. I am united with the King of kings and Lord of lords who, with sovereign grace and authority, leads me to that final chapter.

When I think of the mystery of transformation, I cannot help but be reminded of the story of the good Samaritan. Three men traveled the same road, heading in the same direction. But though in these physical qualities they were equal, the difference in their spiritual maturity was phenomenal. The mystery of transformation is that Jesus Christ meets us where we are and takes us to where he is.

If you have never come to Christ initially, inviting him into your heart as Lord and Savior of your life, you are missing the chance to let God begin that work of maturing grace in your life. The Scriptures say, "Behold, he cometh with clouds; and every eye shall see him, and they also which pierced him: and all kindreds of the earth shall wail because of him. Even so, Amen" (Rev. 1:7). "Now unto him that is able to

keep you from falling, and to present you faultless before the presence of his glory with exceeding joy, to
the only wise God, our Saviour, be glory and majesty,
dominion and power, both now and ever. Amen" (Jude
24-25).

9
The Mystery of
His Will

Blessed be the God and Father of our Lord Jesus Christ, who hath blessed us with all spiritual blessings in heavenly places in Christ: according as he hath chosen us in him before the foundation of the world, that we should be holy and without blame before him in love: having predestinated us unto the adoption of children by Jesus Christ to himself, according to the good pleasure of his will, to the praise of the glory of his grace, wherein he hath made us accepted in the beloved. In whom we had redemption through his blood, the forgiveness of sins, according to the riches of his grace; wherein he hath abounded toward us in all wisdom and prudence; having made known unto us the mystery of his will, according to his good pleasure which he hath purposed in himself: That in the dispensation of the fullness of times he might gather together in one all things in Christ, both which are in heaven, and which are on earth; even in him: In whom also we have obtained an inheritance, being predestinated according to the purpose of him who worketh all things after the counsel of his own will: That we should be to the praise of his glory, who first trusted in Christ (Eph. 1:3-9).

The key verses and key phrases are verse 5, "the good pleasure of his will"; verse 9, "the mystery of his will"; and verse 11, "the counsel of his own will." God is not "It." God is "he" and "he" is "him." "He" is not some "thing"; He is "somebody" and a "someone." God has personality and all the faculties of personality which include knowledge, emotion, and will. He has a will. The key verse is verse 9: "Having made known unto us the mystery of his will." So that which God has purposed, which is not part of many wills, is his exclusive will.

As we study the mystery of the will of God, we begin with a positive approach because the apostle made it clear that God has made known unto us the mystery of his will. We have all the tools to unlock this mystery. This is one of the mysteries of God that we need not say, "I can't understand that one until I get to heaven." The mystery of the will of God may be known to all.

By the "will of God" we simply mean, what's God up to. Why did God make me? Why the cross? After a rebellious world was once wiped out by a flood, why a second chance? Why didn't God send us spinning into the oblivion and obscurity of a thousand hells with no chance for reconciliation, no grace, and no opportunity of redemption? He could have dropped the curtain the first time you and I committed our first sin! But God is up to something. God has a plan, an idea, an overall program for the whole world. It is the mystery of his will.

We have already discussed the mystery of glorification. The purpose of God in the glorification of the believer is that God, having foreknown me, did predestinate me to be conformed to the image of his Son.

Nothing, but nothing, shall separate me from the final accomplishment of that fact. God wants to bring me into conformity to the image of his Son, so that when I am remade in my final state, I will be like Christ. Every believer in heaven will be like Jesus, and there'll be more for the Father to love. Please note! If Romans and its doctrine of glorification is the mystery of the purpose of God, then Ephesians 1 is the theological aspect of that mystery. Romans 8 tells us how glorification happens, as we move from foreknowledge to predestination, from call to conversion, from justification to sanctification, to glorification. But Ephesians 1 tells how glorification is accomplished in the mind of God from the foundation of the world. The singular purpose of God, to bring many unto adoption is the same thing as the *will* of God in Ephesians.

Look in Ephesians 1:5. "The adoption of children" (we are adopted into the family of God—we are children of God—we are sons of God—we are brothers and sisters with Jesus Christ (verse 10). "That in the dispensation of the fulness of times he might gather together in one all things in Christ," (all in Christ—all one with Christ—all like Christ (verse 12). "That we should be to the praise of his glory who first trusted in Christ." So what is the will of God? It is to bring, by trusting in Jesus Christ, all people together into the likeness of the unity and oneness that is the centrality of Jesus Christ. One world, one body, one building, one bride, one family all in Jesus Christ. That is the mystery of his will.

That is the wonder of it, the beauty of it, the joy of it. But the theology must be understood in four

ingredients. God's will is accomplished in four ways:
(1) predestination is by foreknowledge
(2) adoption is by grace
(3) redemption is by blood
(4) unity is by Christ

Predestination Is by Foreknowledge

The first ingredient is predestination, that which God decided before the world to do and which will come to a full reality only after the world is finished. It is the foreknowledge and prior plan of God. Look again at Ephesians 1:3-6. "Blessed be the ... Father of our Lord Jesus Christ, who hath blessed us with all spiritual blessings in heavenly places in Christ: According as he hath chosen us in him before the foundation of the world." Before the world began, God had in mind to bring many unto adoption and to transform them into his image. We must identify what God planned before the world began and which must be consummated after the world is finished.

Three things in this Scripture passage speak to us of God's prior plan. "He hath chosen us in him before the foundation of the world" (v. 4). Before the world was, God chose you. God predetermined to select you as an object of his grace. He then predestinated us unto adoption" (v. 5). He predetermined to love us and to call us. All of this is done before. Toward what is our selection and adoption moving in the overall, single-minded, will of God? We are moving toward being conformed to the image of God's son.

Look at verse 3, "Who hath blessed us with all spiritual blessings in heavenly places in Christ," and verse 4, "That we should be holy and without blame before him in love." Christians cannot so sin as to be lost. We cannot take ourselves out of our Father's hand. He has chosen us before the foundation of the world to present us without blame, unto himself. The will of God is going to be done. "Unto the adoption of children ... [we are adopted into the family of God, v. 5] he hath made us accepted in the beloved" (v. 6). Before the foundation of the world, then, there was the choice of God in predestination. When we are born, the process continues. God calls us and we respond to his gift of salvation. In the future, we will be seated in heavenly places, perfect before God as his adopted children, accepted in the Beloved.

So you see, your conversion was not an accident. Before Venus, Mars, and Pluto ever existed, God knew you. God loved you. God chose you. God planned to provide for your salvation. But does that mean that God makes arbitrary choices? He says, "Whosoever will" may come. And yet he says, I will harden whom I will and have mercy on whom I will. How can we harmonize the sovereignty of God to choose whom he will with the free will of people to respond to God? We can't? It is, like the Trinity, a mystery. I really feel that Paul's commentary on Romans answers that question for us when it goes back to the foreknowledge of God. Paul told us who the people were that God predestinated. "For whom he did foreknow, he also did predestinate" (v. 29). Foreknew what? God knew our choice. He knew we would respond to the gospel, therefore, he moved heaven and earth to make it possible for us to respond.

Admittedly, there are persons who may never have a chance to respond to the gospel and God knows they wouldn't respond if they heard it. But God knows who will respond and planned to create the opportunity for us to respond so that he can begin the process that ends in glorification and brings us to heaven to be like him.

Adoption Is by Grace

Not only is predestination by foreknowledge, but adoption, the result of predestination, is by grace. "Having predestinated us unto the adoption of children by Jesus Christ to himself, according to the good pleasure of his will, To the praise of the glory of his grace, wherein he hath made us accepted in the beloved. In whom we have redemption through his blood, the forgiveness of sins, according to the riches of his grace." God has predestined us to be his adopted children by Jesus Christ. That has been his will. We have responded to that will to the praise and glory of his grace. Before we boast of a self-centered theology that says, "I decided for God and so God decided for me," We must remember that the whole adoptive process is the result of the *grace of God.*

What is grace? It is unmerited favor. It is what we don't deserve. It is what our righteousness can't buy because we have no righteousness. The fact that God created a process in which we would respond to each other is all the manifestation of grace. Listen to John 1:16. "Of his fulness have all we received, and grace for grace." Some modern translations (NIV, RSV) say "grace upon grace." Grace upon grace—no. It is "of his fulness have all we received, and grace for

grace." It means that God gives us grace to respond to
his grace. Therefore, it is all grace, unmerited favor.
Jesus Christ not only died on the cross to provide our
salvation, he not only tugged at our hearts to respond
to salvation but also he gave us the grace to respond to
his grace! What caused the love of God to put in our
hearts the capacity to respond to his grace? His grace!
You cannot respond to God's grace unless he gives you
the grace to do it. The grace to respond to God's grace
makes all of grace. There's no room in the Christian
gospel for any flesh or glory in God's presence. While
it is true that we, by grace, respond to that which he
predetermined by foreknowledge, it is also true that
the price of grace is not cheap. The basis of grace, the
cross, brings us to the third ingredient of the will of
God.

Redemption Is by Blood

Grace means "free" but it doesn't mean cheap. It
cost God everything. "In whom we have redemption
through his blood, the forgiveness of sins, according to
the riches of his grace" (Eph. 1:7). This simple statement is one of the most profoundly important ones we
will ever understand. Grace—unmerited favor, blessing, and goodness—is free, but it isn't cheap! Grace
was accomplished at the greatest price the world has
ever known: the death of the Son of God "in whom we
have redemption through his blood."

Unity Is by Jesus Christ

Our consummate experience of union and relationship to God in heaven is through Jesus Christ.
That in the dispensation of the fulness of times he

might gather together in one all things in Christ, both which are in heaven, and which are on earth; even in him: In whom also we have obtained an inheritance, being predestinated according to the purpose of him who worketh all things after the counsel of his own will: That we should be to the praise of his glory, who first trusted in Christ (Eph. 1:10-12). For billions of year, there was unity in heaven. Lucifer rebelled and declared war on God and was banished from heaven. God would preserve heavenly unity. But rebellion came to earth, and there is disunity everywhere—in the world, society, the home.

Jesus taught us to pray, "Thy will be done in earth, as it is in heaven." In Ephesians 1, Paul spoke of the unity of the Gentiles and Jews in Jesus Christ. God's goal is unity everywhere. The Arab and the Jew, the black and the white, the rich and the poor, the East and the West will all come together in Jesus Christ. The only way this world is ever going to know unity is in the unity of Jesus Christ. God was in Christ reconciling the world to himself! Ours is a schizophrenic society that cannot be united by human will. The world can never be reconciled to itself until it is reconciled to God's wonderful self. In Christ all things will be complete.

In the fullness of time, in the new heaven and the new earth toward which we are moving, the sons and daughters of God will be made in the image of his Son. Old things will be passed away, and all things will become new. The fellowship of unity is the consummate will of God. John's statement, "We shall be like him; for we shall see him as he is," shall be accomplished by our fellowship in and with the Lord Jesus Christ.

Predestination is by foreknowledge. Adoption is by grace. Redemption is by blood. Unity is by Jesus Christ. This is the mystery of God's will. God, having foreknown me, did predestine me to be conformed to the image of his Son; all things are working together to produce this. Nothing, but nothing, shall separate me from the final accomplishment of that final state. I shall live in heaven in perfect fellowship with all Christians, who themselves are made perfect, in the perfect image of his perfect self.

The redemption of the world to oneness in Christ is Ephesians' "will of God" as it is Romans' "purpose of God." God's will is accomplished by redemption, by grace, and by reconciliation through the blood.

10
The Mystery of
Israel's Rejection

I say the truth in Christ, I lie not, my conscience also bearing me witness in the Holy Ghost, That I have great heaviness and continual sorrow in my heart. For I could wish that myself were accursed from Christ for my brethren, my kinsmen according to the flesh: ... As it is written, Behold, I lay in Sion a stumblingstone and rock of offence: and whosoever believeth on him shall not be ashamed. Brethren, my heart's desire and prayer to God for Israel is, that they might be saved. For I bear them record that they have a zeal of God, but not according to knowledge. For they being ignorant of God's righteousness, and going about to establish their own righteousness, have not submitted themselves unto the righteousness of God. . . . What then? Israel hath not obtained that which he seeketh for; but the election hath obtained it, and the rest were blinded (According as it is written, God hath given them the spirit of slumber, eyes that they should not see, and ears that they should not hear;) unto this day. And David saith, Let their table be made a snare, and a trap, and a stumblingblock, and a recompence unto them: Let their eyes be darkened, that they may not see, and bow down their back alway (Rom. 9:1-3,33; 10:1-3; 11:7-10).

According to Paul, Israel is blind. Though one day "Israel shall be saved," "blindness in part is happened to Israel, until the fulness of the Gentiles come in." The time of her turning is not yet. She is, and has been through the centuries, blind to her own Messiah, the Lord Jesus.

The mystery of Israel's rejection is not specifically called a mystery in Scripture, but the obvious nature of its existence must be dealt with as a mystery. Neither the word *trinity* nor the word *rapture* are used in the Scriptures, but their reality is taught, nontheless. Let us examine six characteristics of the mystery of Israel's rejection.

Israel's Identity

Paul said that "they are not all Israel, which are of Israel." Twice in his letters to the churches of Asia Minor in Revelation, the Lord Jesus refers to the false Jews as the "synagogue of Satan." And who are these false Jews, these people of Israel who are not the true Israel? They are the Jews who reject their own Messiah. A Jew who receives Jesus Christ as Savior becomes a Jew in the truest sense, not merely a convert to Christianity. Jesus was of the Jews and first and foremost the Savior of his own people. Only after the Jews rejected Jesus was the gospel offered the Gentile world.

Spiritually speaking, then, the only real Jews, according to the New Testament, are the Hebrew Christians.

A further identity crisis occurs at the point of lost

national identity taught by some. Herbert W. Arm-
strong and also the "British Israelites" teach, in part,
that the identity of the real Jews is lost today. The two
and one-half tribes who stayed beyond Jordan are said
to have migrated to England, where David's throne
has now become the throne of the queen of England.
This theory says that no real Jews exist in the world
today, and those who occupy the land of Israel now
and who exist over the world claiming to be Jews are
phonies.

Sound biblical scholarship makes obvious the rejection of such a theory. If there are no real Jews, how
can Israel exist as a nation, as it has since 1948? Israel
must exist as a nation to receive the Messiah when he
returns. In Genesis 15, God specifically outlined the
land of Israel which will be inhabited by the descendants of Abraham when King Jesus returns to occupy
the throne promised by the angel (Luke 1:32-33) and
temporarily occupied by the wicked one (2 Thess.
2:3-4). These events shall precipitate the battle of
Armageddon, the final great battle of the world to rid
it of evil and usher in the millennial reign of Christ.

The identity of these people called Jews is well
documented and may be easily traced through history,
though they have gone by three names: Hebrews,
Israelites, and Jews. Abraham was the first person to
be called a Hebrew. The word *Hebrew* comes from the
word *havair*, which means those who came out. The
enemies of Israel, frightened by the stories of their
deliverance from Egypt and the powerful crossing at
the Red Sea, often cried, "The Havairs are coming."

Since there are only 950 words in the Hebrew language, words and names became powerful instruments as conveyors of truth. When Jacob had his personality changed, God fittingly changed Jacob's name to "Israel," "Prince with God." Since Israel was the father of the heirs who would bear the names of the twelve tribes of Israel, the Hebrews quite naturally began to be called "the sons of Israel"—hence Israelites, then simply "Israel."

When the Assyrians carried the ten tribes of the North into captivity in BC 700, the most prominent of the two remaining tribes was the tribe of Judah. From Judah, came the nickname Jew, which has stuck to this day.

Israel's Election or Selection

The Jews are called the chosen people. The psalmist described them as "his peculiar treasure." Herein lies a difficult problem—attempting to witness to Jewish people about the Lord Jesus Christ.

As bearers of the name "chosen people," the Jews often think they have an inside track. To answer the question why they were chosen, one must ask, chosen to do what? Chosen to be what? Most Jewish people think they are automatically in a covenant relationship with God to be saved personally and/or nationally with no further need of a Savior to die for them.

Why God did not choose Africans, Italians, or Texans is open to speculation. But to understand the concept of "the chosen people," we must focus our attention on what they were chosen to do and to be. Perhaps God saw a kind of strict and structured fierceness about Israelites' commitment to things that he liked.

Perhaps there was an identity with the soil, a kind of agragian toughness, that would give them the ability to survive. Perhaps they were chosen for this reason or that. But that they were chosen is beyond question. Precisely what they were chosen to do, however, is of utmost importance. They were chosen to be the human instrument through which the gospel would come.

The prophets were Jewish, the Law was Jewish, the Scriptures are Jewish, the ceremonies were Jewish. The Christ, himself, was a Jew. The Scriptures make it clear that these people are sinners just as much as the Gentiles, that they, too, must have their sins atoned for by faith in the shed blood of Christ. John the Baptist was referred to the entire system of ceremonial law and sacrifices when he introduced Jesus: "Behold the Lamb of God, which taketh away the sin of the world" (John 1:29).

Paul's greatest statement about the privilege of Israel to bear the gospel to the world is:

For I could wish that myself were accursed from Christ for my brethren, my kinsmen according to the flesh: Who are Israelites; to whom pertaineth the adoption, and the glory, and the covenants, and the giving of the law, and the service of God, and the promises; Whose are the fathers, and of whom as concerning the flesh Christ came, who is over all, God blessed for ever. Amen (Rom. 9:3-5).

Israel's Persecution

Why have the Jews suffered so much through the centuries? As the bearers of the gospel, unwitting conspirators with God though they may be, it would appear that they deserved to be the best loved peoples of history. But precisely the opposite is the truth. Perhaps the world's antagonism toward the Jews is that they have often been instruments of God's judgment upon Gentile nations, as witnessed by the entire book of Joshua and Judges.

However, these same Gentile nations served as God's instrument of judgment upon the Jews during their sojourns into idolatry. Who can forget the plot against Israel by wicked Haman or the slaughter at Masada or that of the Romans under Antiochus Epiphanes. Where in the annals of history is there anything to compare with Hitler's slaughter of six million Jews in the gas chambers of Buchenwald and Auschwitz? Not to mention four thousand years of hatred between the sons of Isaac and the sons of Ishmael, erupting at this very moment in the Arab-Israeli world.

The prophet Zechariah warned that the time will come when all nations will come against Israel. The only force that could unite the nations of the world in a confederation behind the Arab block nations is their oil. And the main thing the Arabs are interested in is Jerusalem. This may well be that which occasions the coming of all nations against Israel.

Israel's Preservation

The Lord promised that "no weapon that is formed against thee shall prosper." Repeatedly, Israel has come to the brink of annihilation only to be rescued by God and survive, even to this very hour. All of the nations of the world cannot survive against Israel and will, in fact, one day be slaughtered by droves in the valley of Megiddo sixty miles north of Jerusalem. God will fight for Israel. She is still his special treasure. She will be intact when he comes. "So all Israel shall be saved." As they moan and wail and "look on him whom they pierced." At last, 144,000 of them will likely be evangelists who will fan out across the world and declare the gospel to the unbelieving Gentile nations.

Israel's Blindness

In light of what has been presented, the Jews, for the most part, rejected Jesus as Messiah to this hour?

They are a proud people. They think they are special because they are chosen, but they do not understand what they were chosen to be. They were chosen to be the instrument of God to bring the gospel of Jesus Christ to the world. When Jesus came, they rejected him. They are unaware of their own purpose and proud in their condition. It is not easy to win Jewish people to Christ. A haze of spiritual blindness hangs over their eyes. During the past ten years, we have seen many more than ten thousand persons come to Christ in our First Baptist Church of Houston. How many of this number were Jews? About twenty.

Saul of Tarsus was so blinded to spiritual truth, though he thought himself to be a spiritual man, that God had to knock him down literally in a dazzling display of brilliant light to get his attention. When Hyman Appelman, the brilliant Hebrew-Christian evangelist, believed in Jesus, his own parents had a funeral and buried his memory. To the day he died, they would not visit him or eat with him. Israel's blindness is getting worse. In the mysterious combination of pride in themselves and ignorance about themselves, Israel is slipping farther away from God.

It would probably surprise you to know that no more than 10 percent of the Jews in Israel today attend synagogue, and a large percentage of them are atheists. In Jerusalem in 1972, I asked a young Jewish intellectual how she would recognize her Messiah when he came. "Oh," she said, "the Messiah is already here. The Messiah is not a person. It is the state of Israel itself. The fact that we are in Israel as a people means that we are in the messianic reign." What a pity that most young Jews inhabiting the land of Israel today are not even looking for a personal Messiah.

The Jews are blind because they will not listen to their own Scriptures. How could one read Isaiah, chapter 53 and miss the Lord Jesus Christ?

Who hath believed our report? and to whom is the arm of the Lord revealed? For he shall grow up before him as a tender plant, and as a root out of a dry ground: he hath no form nor comeliness; and when we shall see him, there is no beauty that we should desire him. He is despised and rejected of men; a man of sorrows, and acquainted with grief: and we hid as it were our faces from him; he was despised, and we esteemed him not. Surely he hath borne our griefs, and carried our sorrows: yet we did esteem him stricken, smitten of God, and afflicted. But he was wounded for our transgressions, he was bruised for our iniquities: the chastisement of our peace was upon him; and with his stripes we are healed. All we like sheep have gone astray; we have turned every

one to his own way; and the Lord hath laid on him the iniquity of us all. He was oppressed, and he was afflicted, yet
he opened not his mouth: he is brought as a lamb to the
slaughter, and as a sheep before her shearers is dumb, so he
openeth not his mouth. He was taken from prison and from
judgment: and who shall declare his generation? for he was
cut off out of the land of the living: for the transgression of
my people was he stricken. And he made his grave with the
wicked, and with the rich in his death; because he had done
no violence, neither was any deceit in his mouth. Yet it
pleased the Lord to bruise him; he hath put him to grief:
when thou shalt make his soul an offering for sin, he shall
see his seed, he shall prolong his days, and the pleasure of
the Lord shall prosper in his hand. He shall see of the travail
of his soul, and shall be satisfied: by his knowledge shall my
righteous servant justify many; for he shall bear their iniquities. Therefore will I divide him a portion with the great,
and he shall divide the spoil with the strong; because he hath
poured out his soul unto death: and he was numbered with
the transgressors: and he bare the sin of many, and made in-
tercession for the trangressors (Isa. 53).

*The Jews are blind because they do not recognize
the coming of Messiah as a two-fold coming.* The tradi-
tional argument of the Jew is that Jesus could not be
the Savior because there was no peace on earth when
he was here. The reign of Messiah is to be a reign of
peace on earth. But what the Scriptures teach, and
what Jews habitually refuse to accept, is that the coming of the Messiah is two-fold. The two-fold nature of
his coming is necessitated by the characteristic of that
which keeps us from having peace, sin. Before the
Messiah, then, could bring peace on earth, he had to
deal with the problem of sin.

The Messiah's coming, therefore, is twofold. He

will come a second time to reign over the earth in a
thousand years of peace. We agree that the coming of
Messiah must be a reign of peace, but that is in the future. It was in his first coming to die on the cross that
Jesus dealt with that which alone makes peace possible: his victory at Calvary over sin, the devil, death,
hell, and the grave. There will be peace on earth and
must be peace on earth, but until that time, there can
still be individual islands of peace on earth as men and
women enthrone him King of kings in their hearts.

Israel's Final Restoration

Paul's dynamic statement on this matter is his
promise, "So all Israel shall be saved" (Rom. 11:26).
God is working on a perfect timetable and his plan is
running according to schedule. First, the gospel came
to Israel, and they rejected it. Secondly, it was offered
to the Gentiles. Thirdly, when the last Gentile has
been converted and the Gentile age completed, Christ
will come in glory, and the remaining Israel will be
saved.

Paul spoke clearly to the mystery of Israel's temporary blindness until the dispensation of Gentile
evangelism is complete.

For I would not, brethren, that ye should be ignorant of this
mystery, lest ye should be wise in your own conceits; that
blindness in part is happened to Israel, until the fulness of
the Gentiles be come in. And so all Israel shall be saved: as it
is written, There shall come out of Sion the Deliverer, and
shall turn away ungodliness from Jacob (Rom. 11:25-26).

"Hath God cast away his people? God forbid" (Rom. 11:1).

In that day will I make the governors of Judah like an hearth of fire among the wood, and like a torch of fire in a sheaf; and they shall devour all the people round about, on the right hand and on the left: and Jerusalem shall be inhabited again in her own place, even in Jerusalem. The Lord also shall save the tents of Judah first, that the glory of the house of David and the glory of the inhabitants of Jerusalem do not magnify themselves against Judah. In that day shall the Lord defend the inhabitants of Jerusalem; and he that is feeble among them at that day shall be as David; and the house of David shall be as God, as the angel of the Lord before them. And it shall come to pass in that day, that I will seek to destroy all the nations that come against Jerusalem. And I will pour upon the house of David, and upon the inhabitants of Jerusalem, the spirit of grace and of supplications: and they shall look upon me whom they have pierced, and they shall mourn for him, as one mourneth for his only son, and shall be in bitterness for him, as one that is in bitterness for his firstborn (Zech. 12:6-10).

Israel's blindness is temporary. She who has ears to hear will hear; She whose eyes were blinded—will see. When? Only when the last Gentile is saved: the Gentile bride completed, the church caught out, the tribulation finished, and Christ returns in glory with all the saints and holy angels. Paul exhorted each believer to join him in prayer for Israel's salvation. "Brethren, my heart's desire and prayer to God for Israel is, that they might be saved" (Rom. 10:1).

The promise of God appears to be that all of remaining Israel will be saved when Christ returns in glory, but what of the millions who have died from

Abraham until that hour outside of the faith? Ours is not to speculate the theological implications of Israel's final restoration but to throw ourselves, at this moment, into the battle of winning to Christ millions, both Jew and Gentile, who are perishing daily without the Lord Jesus Christ.

He who promised to "bless them that bless thee, and curse him that curseth thee" (Gen. 12:3) will certainly reward those who attempt to win to him these special people whom our Lord chose and loves so dearly.